Everything divided by 21 million

Knut Svanholm

Edited by Jeff Booth, Mel Shilling and Niko Laamanen

KONSENSUS NETWORK

Edited by Jeff Booth, Mel Shilling and Niko Laamanen

Infinity key art by @FractalEncrypt

Cover design and typesetting by Niko Laamanen

ISBN 978-9916-6973-1-3 Hardcover

    978-9916-697-19-1 Paperback

    978-9916-697-20-7 E-book

KONSENSUS NETWORK ★ https://konsensus.network

I dedicate this book to my fellow bitcoiners, including but not limited to FractalEncrypt, Ioni Appelberg, Guy Swann, Jeff Booth, Volker Herminghaus, Daniel Prince and Hodlonaut

I couldn't have done a 21 millionth of this without you guys

Contents

FOREWORD

Everything is first an idea, competing for our attention, actions, and time. A random idea to meet someone I had only known through Twitter, Knut Svanholm, turned into the most incredible evening of dinner, drinks, and playing guitar with our families in Southern Spain. An instant and deep connection was formed. These interactions change us, often without our realization. Wherever it goes, I suspect it was only the start of a long friendship that all started with an idea.

We are idea machines. Good ideas, mediocre ideas, bad ideas — our entire world is made up of them. A matrix of thoughts governs how we interact with others, our economy, and our system(s) of governance. The chair you're sitting in competed against all other ideas, chair formats, and companies creating chairs to win your attention and purchase. Similar to the car you drive or the smartphone you use. Free speech is an idea. So is communism. We become so wed to our ideas that we often become defined by them. Because of this, they are powerful in uniting us, dividing us… or in controlling us. It is our choice which ideas are right to us, and life reflects those choices.

Individually, our thoughts and actions form our own reality, and collectively they roll up and form our shared reality. From our narrow view of what we consider an accurate representation of the world, we fail to see that others live in a completely different reality that they also deem accurate. We can easily see in others where their ideas may be holding them back, but we completely fail to see the same thing in ourselves. We are so sure in our ideas that we'll fight to protect them, replacing reasoning and logic with emotion to prove our point, which allows us to be easily fooled. In our attempt to defend our ideas at one level, we miss natural incongruences at the foundational level that might be driving them. One example is simultaneously believing in free markets while advocating for Central Bankers to provide liquidity to protect asset prices or the stock market. We have a hard time connecting the dots and seeing the cognitive dissonance.

We cannot predict when a new idea or truth shatters our previous set of beliefs and replaces them with something that works better. We'll fight something for years, only to change our minds entirely in an instant. Once we see it, we can't unsee it. Worse still, from our new enlightenment, we might ridicule others who can't see the new truth. The process takes time, often generations, to weave throughout the world. I often imagine what society felt like to Galileo. When looking at the night sky, he realized that the Earth rotated around the Sun, but it was considered absurd and heretical to the Catholic Church and teaching.

Regardless of the time, these "ideas" are humanity's individual and collective force and consciousness. Competing to find better ways, they improve the human experience as a result. You could consider these ideas learning. Our intelligence as a species always has been, and is today, fundamentally a collective growth of information-driven from this competition of ideas.

Chaotic, messy, disorderly. New ideas must compete with previously held beliefs that have hardened in our minds. We let our grasp of them go one finger at a time, and because we make predictions from our current reality, it's hard for us to imagine how one small change might cascade to others. So, when an idea challenges a previously held belief, there is a high probability that we will either ignore it or fight it instead of investigating it for its merits.

In economics, that process describes *Creative Destruction*, a paradoxical term first coined by Joseph Schumpeter in 1942 to describe how Capitalism works in a free market. Entrepreneurs innovate and create value for society — and that value gained by society also often "destroys" the former monopoly power or "idea." The former monopoly typically either ignores or fights the new idea. That process and its importance are at the center of how modern economies have evolved and given rise to most of the benefits to the society we take for granted today. New winners become so valuable that they disrupt existing market power or structures. Driven from a near-constant flow of innovative entrepreneurs with bold ideas and the capital backing them that challenge the status quo and are only successful, "if" they create value for society (us).

For the process to work, failure is critical! Both for entrepreneurs and the capital in them whose business doesn't work, and for legacy businesses that get disrupted by them, if their innovation brings better value to society. And while failure is difficult, preventing it is far worse because it disrupts the delicate balance of the free market. What starts a seemingly small intervention eventually becomes encoded into a distorted form of Capitalism, cascading to ever-escalating intervention and control to protect the overall market from collapsing. False stability is replaced with growing instability as true market signals evaporate and social constructs decay. Along this path, it is not only the free market that is lost.

Remember, the free market is made up of these ideas. They are us. The sum of our thoughts and actions trying to stand out from other ideas, with an intention to deliver value to others. They form the economy because we choose these new ideas, or we do not, depending on the value they provide to us. We can choose to limit ideas, suppress them, destroy them in the name of control, but as we do, we in turn, limit our own potential.

At a higher level of abstraction than the free market, these actions also form the system by which we govern: to allow the proliferation of ideas to emerge. When we reach into free markets to control them, we distort them. In the short term, with a backdrop of competition for jobs, growth, protection of markets, these decisions usually win accolades from the public and ensure votes. They are popular, but at their core, they lead to some people, industries, or countries winning unfairly at the expense of others. This could be by favoring one company over another domestically or in nations protecting their vital industries from competition. It doesn't matter. Market protection spreads and intensifies as it robs the free market of both labor and capital. *Malinvestments* rise. Structurally, those choices must lead away from our choices and towards an ever-increasing consolidation of power. While that might look like wilful neglect or bad intent, the primary driver is just a system with reinforcing negative feedback loops attempting to protect the status quo and save the system — which would otherwise fail. Greater centralization of control to attempt to stave off the inevitable collapse intrudes further on the free market. As market participants understand how the game is played, more race in for their share of the action. As the distortions escalate, people literally vote away their individual rights and freedoms in favor of protection by the state and centralization. They are fully convinced that the free market is to blame for the rising inequality, division, and societal chaos even though these are predictable consequences of abandoning it.

This is why bitcoin is such an important idea. History proves that if money can be controlled to give an advantage to some over others, it will be. By removing that ability, bitcoin provides a network transfer from a system unable to fix itself, to a system that can. A bridge from a system on a path to a dystopian future to a future of hope.

As the network emerges, the more people who use it and build to it, it continues to increase its value to everyone else, accelerating adoption. Sure, those early in bitcoin hold more of the wealth, as it should be in a free market where they out-predicted others, but importantly, they don't hold more power. In time, the only way to accumulate more bitcoin is by providing value to others, measured by them, in a free market. Coercion is replaced by cooperation as people come to realize that control of others through a monetary network like bitcoin requires paying them in bitcoin and therefore losing control.

Prices falling by extension of the value we provide to others becomes natural. This accelerates as technology continues to do more of our work. Incentives become aligned as we look back with bewilderment that we ever lived in a system where prices were manipulated to rise. We realize a truth that was hidden from our view. Abundance in money = Scarcity in everything else, and conversely, Scarcity in money = Abundance everywhere else. Or as Knut so eloquently describes...

Everything divided by 21 million.

It happens over time, as all new ideas that compete with old ones do. Chaotic, messy, disorderly. But I suspect it is inevitable as more people come to understand its value. The value increases and it becomes harder to ignore. Because the truth is, the system is us. Each of our actions in choosing, in turn, changes our world. It is how ideas we once couldn't see turn into reality. One person at a time.

Jeff Booth, March 2022

PRELUDE

Imagine any species advancing along the path from cave-dwelling to interstellar travel. How would they go about it? Once upon a time, there was such a species. A type of primate who loved to categorize things, label them, and put them in neat little boxes. They called themselves "humans" and other primates "apes." Later they discovered that they share most of their genes with these apes. These humans claimed to be "alive" and "conscious," even though they couldn't clearly define these words. They experienced time and theorized about its relationship with the other dimensions they knew of, namely the three spatial dimensions. Yet they hadn't figured out what time was nor how to value it correctly. Some assumed they had a limited amount of it on this Earth and behaved accordingly. Some didn't even care to give time a single thought and acted as if it was an abundant resource. Some believed in one or more supernatural beings. Some thought that some humans had a divine right to rule over others. None of them knew what was really going on. In an early effort to organize time amongst themselves, they invented a new way of thinking about it. They started to trade time for consumables. They named this new means of interacting with each other "working." Soon after that, they realized they could give each other stuff in exchange for other things. They could trade with one another. Three goats for a cow, for instance. They could also specialize in different skills and help each other by exchanging favors. By doing so, they could count on their neighbor doing their part and allow society to form and grow. A haircut could be traded for an evening of babysitting, for instance. Shortly after that, someone pointed out that there's no easy way to divide a cow into three parts. At least not if you intended on keeping it alive during the process. Also, no one (except maybe the monks) wanted half a haircut.

This lack of divisibility in most goods and services posed a problem, especially for those with only one goat or cow to spare. Therefore, humans had to invent a way to track what belonged to whom. Be it cows or goats, haircuts, pots, or spears. Enter the ledger. A ledger is a book or collection of accounts in which humans record transactions. Historical findings point to ledgers as the first type of writings with numbers that humans ever produced. These ledgers enabled early societies to track who owned what and owed what to whom. The earliest known ledgers are pictographic tablets. The Mesopotamians used them over 5000 years ago.

Another thing that humans invented to keep track of ownership was the "token." They started to exchange tokens, like seashells or precious stones, representing a particular value. These tokens were very local phenomena at first. As time passed, coins forged of precious metals replaced these early forms of money. At first, these were just pieces of a particular metal of a specific weight. Soon enough, the self-proclaimed ruler of a geographical area often claimed an exclusive right to issue them. Usually, this was the same sociopath who stole all the land from your ancestors back in the day. The king.

Coins had many advantages over other means of expressing value. They provided a Medium of Exchange to the people, and they kept their value quite well over time. People liked precious metals, it seemed. It was easy to keep track of them and who owned what in the village. Besides this, they offered an excellent Unit of Account for the issuer. This system worked quite well for quite some time. That is until someone had the idea of clipping off little pieces from the edge of the coins to salvage the precious metal. This benefitted the clipper because the coin would still maintain its value through other people's eyes, and the clipper could sell the salvaged metal too. So to him, each coin became worth a little more. This was the birth of counterfeiting. A practice that is still at the core of every government-issued currency today.

But coin-clippers weren't the only ones meddling with money. The coin issuers soon found new ways to increase their position in the developing trading system. While the coin-clippers could lessen the amount of gold or silver in a coin by removing bits from each one that passed through his hands, the issuer could change the contents of every new token from gold and silver to alloys of less expensive metals. This early form of mass debasement enriched the issuer at the expense of everyone else. Despite these inherent flaws, coins continued to provide a means of trading between people for a long time. Until the invention of the bank, that is.

Along with the invention of the bank came the creation of the banknote. A piece of paper stating how much gold and silver a client had deposited into the bank's vault. In other words, how much the bank owed the client. A banker could also lend money from the bank, and then the borrower would pay back the loan plus some interest. Lending provided the banker with a way to make a living. And the banknote gave people a new way of conducting trade. Pretty soon, people started trading these banknotes instead of gold coins. Banknotes didn't weigh as much as coins and were easier to carry. Banknote trading worked fine too for a while, but the banker soon noticed something peculiar about his clients. They never seemed to withdraw all their gold at the same time. His vault was never empty but full of gold at all times.

An idea started to form in the mind of the banker. What if he wrote a receipt for gold that wasn't even in the vault and lent it out to someone? That someone would then have to pay back the loan with interest. As long as the other clients didn't try to withdraw all the gold simultaneously, they probably wouldn't notice. The plan worked, and voilà, fractional reserve banking was born. Fractional reserve banking made the banker extremely wealthy. As he loaned out more receipts for things that didn't exist, the total debt owed to him grew larger and larger. The process increased the demand for even more loans. The total amount owed by society no longer matched the total available capital. When it finally dawned on people that the banker wasn't playing a fair game, they became outraged. They realized that if they all tried to withdraw their gold simultaneously, the banker would have to come clean. Thus, the *bank run* was born. Bank runs put some banks out of business, but it also led the surviving ones to become even more imaginative. They banded together to combat their clients even more aggressively. In doing so, they spawned the birth of the most sinister institution ever known to man—the Central Bank.

A Central Bank functions as a lender of last resort to all the other banks: It can prevent bank runs by bailing out the smaller banks. Even worse, this practice is essential for a fiat monetary system to work at all. Without central banks, people would probably revolt, which would lead to civil wars. As Henry Ford put it, "It is well enough that people of the nation do not understand our banking and monetary system, for if they did, I believe there would be a revolution before tomorrow morning." A central bank also possesses a monopoly on increasing a country's money supply. A way to enrich itself and the state for which it works. In other words, a way to keep the country's citizens in check. Whoever controls the money supply controls the nation. Control of a money printer makes you a demi-god. Control of the master money printer makes you omnipotent. You can start enormous projects without ever having to pay for them. Ill-advised war efforts suddenly become affordable and even lucrative. By diluting the value of everyone else's time and efforts, a Central Bank controls everything.

This is where the species advancing from cave-dwelling to interstellar travel is right now. Inflation is a force that keeps all humans in shackles. It forces us to stay in our hamster's wheel every day to pay off our debts. Currency is created in the same way today as in the early days of fractional reserve banking. But on a much, much bigger scale. The banknotes in your wallet are not receipts for anything. You cannot claim anything back from the bank by turning them in. They are nothing but debt. Every bill in your pocket, every number on your online bank statement, is debt. All fiat money is a promise to pay back a loan backed by an asset that wasn't there in the first place. It is all fraudulent. It is all a scam, and it is all an enormous pyramid scheme. Understanding this is a prerequisite to understanding what is happening in the world right now. Why is there so much civil unrest and so much polarization? Why are governments taking more and more harsh measures to control their populations? During this first half of the 21st century, we're all living through the most critical societal paradigm shift in human history. Hyperbitcoinization. We may have a tumultuous time ahead of us, but it would have been a lot worse without the financial airbag that bitcoin provides.

Bitcoin is a highly potent tool for protecting yourself against inflation. Like all other tools and technologies, it saves you time. Increases your freedom to choose. If it hasn't already, bitcoin will affect you in ways you cannot imagine. What started as a nerdy digital cash experiment has mutated into something much bigger. Today, bitcoin is nothing short of a global spiritual renaissance. A reclamation of the human soul. An exit strategy for anyone tired of the drudgery of a purposeless career. A pathway to morality, cooperation, and self-sovereignty. An actual shot at saving not only ourselves but the planet we live on, too. People all over the globe are changing their ways at a very rapid pace, waking up to this new reality. They're seeing this emergent phenomenon for what it is — the emancipation of humankind. An idea whose time has come. The most unstoppable force there is. An abstract concept that will change everything about you. An agreement between people that connects time, morality, and information. It will affect you in ways you can't even imagine. This book will try to help you understand why and how.

Bitcoin can be understood from many different angles. And people have interpreted what it is in many different ways. You can, of course, understand all the technical aspects of how bitcoin, the open-source program, works. But this knowledge is entirely pointless without understanding the economic theories it is built upon. Without knowledge of the underlying economics, you won't grasp the societal changes bitcoin is about to unleash. Without some understanding of mathematics and game theory, chances are that you're not convinced about bitcoin's functionality. Without knowledge about praxeology and Austrian economics, you might not even be aware of the problems bitcoin solves. But all you have to do to get a little taste of how bitcoin can change your personal philosophy is to get off zero. Owning bitcoin will change you and how you interact with the world around you.

I've been very interested in mathematics, game theory, and philosophy throughout my adult life. And I do believe that understanding first principles requires an understanding of logic. I always wanted to understand economics, but it wasn't until I discovered bitcoin and Austrian economics that the world of finance started to make sense to me. Studying praxeology changed me. I realized that many of my foundational beliefs weren't actually true. It left me wanting to understand more. Once bitcoin happened, it clicked. During my last seven years before writing this book, I pursued a career in the offshore wind industry. Before that, I spent most of my twenties and thirties working as a deck officer on a tall ship sailing around the globe with high school students on board. Before exiting fiat altogether, my most recent position was as a crew manager for a Swedish/Danish shipping company. When I first entered the bitcoin space, I viewed my past career as a disadvantage. But as time passed, I realized that it gave me a unique perspective. I spent a lot of time philosophizing under a starlit sky crossing the Atlantic, and I've visited more than forty countries. I've been through all the different stages of an office career, and I've managed about 250 employees. These jobs and experiences have provided me with a unique set of insights, and I'm more than happy to share them. Bitcoin changed me, and I'm so glad it did.

This book came to be because of a meme. Sometime in July of 2020, I started writing an article about a conundrum in mathematics, *The Banach-Tarsky paradox*, and how it related to bitcoin. I didn't think much of the article but sent it to Citadel 21 magazine anyway, hoping they would publish it soon. I felt a bit sleepy when writing it, and the text seemed to wander off in directions I hadn't planned. But the dream-like state I was in felt comfortable, and I kept on writing. I fell asleep and slept like a baby on the couch when I was done. I didn't think much more of it, and some time passed. It was published in Citadel 21 magazine on the 21st of August 2020. Shortly after that, Guy Swann of the Bitcoin Audible podcast made an audio version of it on his pod. I heard this audio version late one night in Copenhagen, walking to my hotel from a bitcoin meetup and steak dinner. My hotel was near the airport, and the restaurant was in the city center, so I had quite a long way to walk. I didn't mind, and hearing the article after almost forgetting about it was very satisfying. It was a lot better than I remembered, and I felt happy with myself, especially after hearing Guy's commentary on the article. I remember thinking to myself, "Hey, maybe you're onto something here, Knut," as I strolled down the beautiful alleyways between Nyhavn and Amager.

Somewhere in the middle of the article, you can find this passage "Imagine the entire world economy moving into bitcoin. Everything there is, divided by 21 million." This phrase later became the title of a video rendition of the article by Ioni Appelberg, whom I've collaborated with many times. I also tweeted something similar in October 2020, "Imagine, everything there is and everything that will ever be, divided by 21 million. No one understands." Bitcoin Core developer Adam Back retweeted my sentiment, and shortly after that, the phrase quickly gained momentum. People began to add the "infinity divided by 21M" -equation to their Twitter handles, and suddenly, it was everywhere. It had a life of its own. In 2021, I launched a limited edition clothing collection featuring the equation, and Michael Saylor of MicroStrategy tweeted the quote a couple of times. Early in August of the same year, I was one of the speakers at The Bitcoin Standard Conference in Ensenada, Mexico. During my ten days in "the Baha," the idea of "Bitcoin Infinity Day" came up.

Bitcoin Infinity Day celebrates bitcoin's potential to take over the entire world economy. On the 21st of August each year, you stack 21 times your regular daily stack. If you are already *Dollar Cost Averaging* (DCA), it's easy to calculate how much this adds up to. If you stack once a month, divide by thirty and multiply by 21. If you don't have a cyclical Sat stacking plan... Why don't you have a cyclical Sat stacking plan? I announced Bitcoin Infinity Day on Tone Vays' YouTube show in early August 2021. The day itself would happen just two weeks later. It quickly gained momentum and became a thing in the community. Especially when renowned bitcoin artist FractalEncrypt made an art piece in honor of the day. He made 21 "Private Infinity Keys" and auctioned out number eight out of twenty-one on Scarce City[1] — the Lightning-enabled bitcoin auction site. It sold for 1.05 bitcoin, worth about $67.000 at the time. The remaining twenty were given to a group of hand-picked bitcoiners who had told the artist something about bitcoin that he didn't know. There was also a "Public Infinity Key," which you could buy for a limited amount of time — 210 blocks, to be precise. Poetically, the price of these Public Keys went up a certain amount with each passing block.

A part of my personal motivation for writing this book is to keep the equation meme and Bitcoin Infinity Day alive. I want to spread the word as much as I can and contribute to a better future for my children. I genuinely find it satisfying to do so from a meaning-of-life perspective. Bitcoin completely devoured my soul when I discovered it, and it provided me with hope in an otherwise bleak world. Many other bitcoiners have similar stories. Bitcoin changes you more than you can change it. More than anyone can change it. Rules without rulers provide us with a base layer of truth to build everything else on top of. The inner journey that bitcoin motivates you to embark on might be the most fulfilling thing you'll ever do. Even if you don't choose to pursue a career in bitcoin, it will change your behavior.

---

[1] https://scarce.city/

Bitcoin's limited supply cap is the immovable object that enables us all to become an unstoppable force.

The arguments in this book are from the perspective that bitcoin works and that it will continue to work in the future. Even if bitcoin would fail at some point due to some black swan event, I think the discussion about what an absolutely scarce, uncensorable informational asset will do to the way we interact with each other is worth having anyway.

1

TIME

W E'RE all chained to the unforgiving arrow of time. We're born, we live, and we get old. At least that's what we hope will happen. Then we die. And, if we've managed to reproduce, the existential baton is handed over to the next generation. If we're lucky and play our cards well, we can influence several generations. Most people trifle away this opportunity without ever reflecting too much on it. The thoughts of those who change the world live on. Ideas live on their own, and important ones significantly impact every person's life. Imagine life without the wheel, the ability to start a fire, electricity, the internet, or... bitcoin. Those who've understood the importance of the discovery of bitcoin find it intriguing like fire. As helpful as the wheel, as convenient as electricity, and as world-changing as the internet. A remarkable shift in how we live our lives is just around the corner. A fundamental change in the way we organize ourselves. A global social paradigm shift of unprecedented proportions. A new level of civility. An awakening. This discovery is a representation of time itself. It's connected to time in ways of which we've only begun to realize the implications. It's an emergent phenomenon, and it's happening everywhere at once. An idea whose time has come.

Bitcoin's price, that is, the value of the network, reflects this reorganization. It functions as a lagging indicator of people's understanding of the value of their time. The ever-increasing purchasing power of those who hold bitcoin is what this new paradigm is all about. As time goes by, the old systems will lose their significance. Bitcoiners will become more influential, and the pointlessness of our old ways will be more evident over time. We're living through hyperbitcoinization. It's a pretty straightforward process. The power of all the other currencies diminishes over time compared to bitcoin. Time is critical. It's as essential to bitcoin as it is to everything else in our lives. There's a deep connection between how we experience time and value things. A link between our subjective experiences and the objective reality we live in. We can't change the direction of time, but we can change our relationship with it. If we set up a long-term goal for ourselves, we can structure our lives in ways that help us pursue that goal. If we keep the goal in the forefront of our minds, our day-to-day struggle becomes pleasurable. The Schwarzenegger way. Every push-up, every exam we pass, and every penny we make can all be aimed towards the same goal. Most people understand this, but few can articulate their own ultimate goal. More importantly, they don't realize they can figure out a long-term plan during their journey. Hence, they fail. Exercising your body and sharpening your mind will help you regardless of your goal. Becoming more wealthy helps too. Wealth is the sum total of your efforts minus expenditures. What you own, at any moment, is the only hand you can play in the market. Now imagine that someone could dilute the value of your work unilaterally. That they could do so by the push of a button, without your consent or vote? What would society look like? Would people think of long- or short-term goals in such a society? Could they even afford to think long-term?

Your wealth is the sum total of your efforts and expenditures, and you are the sum total of your experiences. Good and bad ones. Dreary, unfulfilling segments of your life also play a part in who you are. They teach you what to avoid and how being unproductive can impact your reality. Your mind evolved over millennia to fit into a group, so naturally, you compare your life to the lives of others. But, don't underestimate the uniqueness of your life. The longer you live, the more unique your personal journey becomes. The more unique skill-sets you acquire, the more valuable you become to others. The basic principles of the free market are still present everywhere. The division of labor works in your favor. Regardless of what political system you live in, your uniqueness determines your value to others. This is true not only for humans but also for technologies, ideas, assets, and everything else. Originality, or scarcity, is crucial to how valuable something is. Availability and demand determine the prices of everything. Make sure you're in short supply. This is as effective as being in high demand. You decide the value of your time. No one else can do it for you. How valuable something is, is a product of the human mind. When more than one mind craves something, that thing generates a price. But whether that price is worth paying or not is for the buyer to decide. Abundant resources don't have prices. Air, for instance, is almost always free. Scarce things are costly. And nothing in the world has a more limited supply than your time on this Earth. It diminishes with every tick of the clock. Your time on this planet becomes even more limited with every word of this you read.

Now think of order and chaos, or entropy. Entropy and time are inexorably linked. The second law of thermodynamics describes the irreversibility of natural processes. Increased entropy is the very thing that distinguishes the future from the past. Entropy gives the unforgiving arrow of time its direction. In this sense, bitcoin adoption functions as a shield against entropy. A way to give humanity more time, if you will. At least on a macro scale. We'll get back to all these concepts later in this book. But for now, try to imagine how much time you have left on this Earth. Try to make a rough estimate. You have a lot of seconds left, but not that many years. Your focus during those seconds will determine the outcome of those years to a large extent. Choose wisely how you spend your days. They're not coming back. Think. Error correct. Enjoy. The time you have on this planet is scarce. So is the total number of bitcoins that will ever exist. This feature alone makes bitcoin the perfect trading tool. Every tool that mankind ever invented saves someone time somewhere. That's the ultimate purpose of tools and technologies. Time-saving is progress. We emancipate ourselves from the drudgery of whatever hamster's wheel we're in by freeing up time. Bitcoins are scarce for all coming generations also, so they can free up time for everyone, forever. Finally, we have a fair way of cooperating with each other. A way to find order in a chaotic world. A signal in the noise. A tool that enables global free trade without interventionism. A set of rules that no one can tamper with. Most people have no idea how powerful this is, but they will learn. Patience is key here. If you own bitcoin, you can afford to be patient.

Every tool and every technology saves someone time, somewhere. One could even argue that everything we assign value to saves us time. We value things because of how much time we predict they can save us. Think of it this way: you can either kill your time or let someone else waste it. There's nothing else to do with it. You're a hunter on the prowl for time to kill. If you own your time, you get the privilege of killing it. If you let others decide what to do with your time for you, you allow others to waste your time. If you want to reclaim the driver's seat of your life, your first priority should be to prevent others from wasting your time. External forces compete to waste your time. First, nature itself destroys your time. Nature forces you to eat, sleep and seek shelter from the elements. For most of us, this means that we have to work. A lot. Then there are other people. Many want to waste your time, too. A lot of them succeed.

Successful time thieves steal time from you without you even noticing, like those in charge of issuing fiat currency. The inflation rate presented to you in mainstream media only reflects a small percentage of what's really going on. Real inflation is always proportional to the increase in the money supply. However, it always comes with a lag, and the closer you are to the money faucet, the more you benefit from this lag. Those closest to the money printers enjoy such modern wonders as negative interest rates and favorable regulations. But all goods go up in price when there's more money around. You cannot create value by pretending that there's more value in the system. Someone somewhere will have to pay the bill sooner or later. No matter what politicians say, there's no way around this.

Another way to look at time is to consider it the only natural resource worth anything. The very definition of economics is the management of scarce resources. Now imagine that you knew that you would live forever. That you were both immortal and indestructible. Imagine that you wouldn't even need to eat. In this hypothetical case, you wouldn't need to act, ever. You could always wait until tomorrow. Postpone everything indefinitely, forever. In such a reality, nothing would be of value to you. With unlimited time on your hands, you wouldn't need to value anything. If time were abundant, everything else would become abundant too. We attach value to goods and services because of the scarcity of human time. In this sense, your time is not only your most precious possession but the only thing you can own. Time which you, yourself, command. Moments in the driver's seat. They are all you have. Bitcoin provides a perfect reflection of this since bitcoins are strictly finite too. Bitcoin is indeed the only asset that can represent the scarcity of your time. And the shortage of everyone else's too. When bitcoins are lost, they're lost forever. But the network's value remains. The fact that their supply is so limited is what makes them valuable. The fact that they're teleportable, uncensorable, and that you can store them in your head doesn't hurt. But their real value lies in the fact that they are finite forever.

Absolute mathematical scarcity was a discovery. Not an invention. This realization is key to understanding bitcoin. The moment you realize what this implies, there's no going back. It is an epiphany. It is what "falling down the rabbit hole" means. One day, someone might suggest an "upgrade" of the protocol that proposes to increase the limit. Anything that would change bitcoin's monetary policy would be detrimental to the project. Almost every node owner knows this. This is why changes to bitcoin's monetary policy can't happen. Sure, bitcoin forks into clones of the real deal every now and then, but these copycats aren't bitcoin. They're not even close. Satoshi named the bitcoin blockchain *the timechain* in many of his notes. Calling it this is an excellent way to separate the real deal from copycats. There's the timechain, and then there are other blockchains. One matters. The others don't.

Bitcoin and time are connected. Bitcoin even has its own definition of time called *block height*. Block height is a location in the timechain defined by how many confirmed blocks precede it. The current block height of the blockchain is a measurement of its current time in existence. In fact, it is bitcoin's own way of measuring time.

Bitcoin's inner clock. Without its own way of measuring time, bitcoin wouldn't work. By now, most people ought to know that the network produces a block every ten minutes, on average. Few understand how this mechanism works and why it is crucial to bitcoin's functionality. There is no such thing as a "digital token." If you think there is, you've misunderstood what a computer does and what information is. In the digital realm, there are only ones and zeroes. Pure, binary information. When you "send" something over the internet, your computer is not "sending" anything. It copies some of the information it holds onto another computer. There's no way of sending information without copying it. Computers can't, and neither can you. If there's a thought in your head and you express it as a sentence, you haven't "sent" anything. The information about what you said is still in your head even after you've said it. The same is even more true for the digital realm. Digital copies are perfect clones of the original information. Computers allow for no loss of information whatsoever. A computer deals in ones and zeroes. Nothing else. A computer is nothing but an enormous, connected set of on/off switches. This means that you can copy everything you do on a computer over and over again as many times as you want. To me, the nature of data and how copyable it was, revealed itself during my childhood. As a kid, I learned how to write a simple program using only PRINT and GOTO on my Commodore 64. I could make the computer write infinite copies of whatever I wanted with these commands. Soon, the TV screen said, "All work and no play makes Jack a dull boy" or something similar. It felt like a profound insight. I had understood something that my parents hadn't. I had understood what "data" was. Understanding the true nature of bitcoin gives me a similar feeling. It took a long time to accept what it was. Something on the internet that wasn't copyable. At first, it sounded as outlandish as a time machine. Could this thing exist for real? I had to investigate further.

So now that we've established that digital tokens do not exist, how does bitcoin work? Bitcoin is a distributed spreadsheet. It is a ledger, a register that records who owns what and when. The "when" is crucial to the ledger as ownership transfers can only happen at specific moments. Remember that if time wasn't scarce, things wouldn't have value, and ownership would be pointless. If a transaction didn't have a "when" attached to it, the network wouldn't be able to verify that it wasn't a copy. In other words, someone could have spent those coins more than once.

Because of this, a ledger needs a way to timestamp each transaction it records. This poses a problem. How can a network of computers sync time? We know that syncing time is crucial for this kind of distributed ledger to work, yet using a central server to keep track of time wouldn't work. That server would be a single point of failure for the network. To be robust enough for immutability, the network would need its own timekeeping mechanism. It couldn't trust an external source. The system needs to be trustless if it is to be peer-to-peer. This is where entropy comes in. As explained above, entropy is what gives time its direction. The bitcoin network takes advantage of this fact and builds its own internal clock. How difficult the next bitcoin block is to find gets adjusted every 2016th block by the system itself. Bitcoin has an internal mechanism for adjusting the difficulty of finding blocks known as the difficulty adjustment algorithm. This algorithm ensures that the same amount of time passes between each block.

A hashing algorithm is another type of algorithm that the network uses. It converts an input data array of a specific kind, here in the form of a bitcoin block, into an output string of characters with a fixed length. A block consists of all proposed transactions plus a random number called a *nonce*. When a miner tries to find the next bitcoin block, he tests different hashes of that block. He tries different nonces to find the next block's hash beginning with a certain number of zeroes. This particular number of zeroes gets decided by the difficulty adjustment algorithm. This might sound complicated, but think of it this way — bitcoin mining is about guessing a number. Guessing this number takes, on average, ten minutes. The greater the number of miners that try to find this number, the more difficult it becomes to do so. This is how the network keeps track of time without relying on outside third parties. It is also how the network rewards the miners who put in the most work to find the next block. The fact that they did is the Proof-of-Work that the system runs on. Because there's no way of faking a hash beginning with that many zeroes (19 at the time of writing). You have to put in the work and prove that you did. One could call this probabilistic timekeeping. Bitcoin is taking entropy and making something useful out of it. Creating order from chaos. A signal from the noise. Using real-world resources to create a numeric representation of time. Building a bridge between subjective value assignments and objective reality. Marrying praxeology and mathematics.

You're not a millionaire in terms of hours. You have way less than a million hours left to live. Let's run some numbers. Each year that passes, you spend 8760 hours. During leap years, you lose 24 more. About a third of all hours you have, you spend sleeping. If you're reading this book, you're probably an adult. Chances are high that you have less than half a million awake hours left. Only you can make those hours count. Only you can decide their value. Whenever you crave a physical *good*, ask yourself why. Will the good save you time or not? Because that is at the core of why you assign value to it. Even the purpose of a Porsche or a Gucci handbag is to save time. People buy luxury goods to signal success to others. In doing so, they hope to save time by climbing the social hierarchies. This can help them get a better job or find a partner from a particular segment of society. The goal is status or power. A power that then can be used to free up time. In this sense, every good is a service. You buy things because of what you can do with them. Realizing the power of time reclamation is a shortcut to a more fulfilling life. That said, there are probably more efficient ways to free up time than buying Gucci bags. Physical things can act as assets or liabilities. If a physical good is desirable and scarce, chances are high that its price will rise over time. Fiat currencies are not finite. As long as new currency units can be created, they can't be. This is one of the reasons why the ratio between assets and money is high for wealthy people. Dollars and Euros lose value over time. Scarce desirable assets don't. If you don't own assets, you lose. Always. This is the main reason the super-wealthy get richer at the expense of everyone else. Remember, inflation is dilution of the value of your time. If we want to "fight poverty," we need to fight inflation. Everyone would thrive without the inflation-driven exploitation of the lower-income classes. Even the super-wealthy would be better off if they allowed others to flourish. A society devoid of time theft would be better for everyone.

2

ALCHEMY

THIS chapter is inspired by a brilliant talk by Jörg Hermsdorf at the Value of Bitcoin conference in 2020 called "The Last Money." His way of framing bitcoin changed my thinking about it a lot, and I'd like to take this opportunity to thank him. The presentation is still available online.[1]

Alchemy was an ancient form of pseudoscience that tried to turn cheap "base" metals into gold. Why gold? Because gold has held its perceived value to humans for at least five thousand years. A cow priced in gold costs more or less the same now as it did in the age of Tutankhamun. Gold happens to have physical properties that make it suitable as a form of money. It is one of two noble, non-radioactive, non-toxic, mononuclidic metals. Mononuclidic means that there's only one natural stable isotope of the element. The other is Rhodium, discovered in 1803 by British physician William Wollaston. Gold has a very high stock-to-flow ratio due to its monetary properties and history. This means that gold's existing stockpile is enormous compared to the inflow of new gold onto the market. Since gold remains somewhat scarce, it can hold its value over long periods. Extracting

---

[1]https://youtu.be/-2RlW7bIe-s

gold from the earth's crust is a very costly process. Thus, an increase in its price doesn't immediately lead to a rise in the production of new gold. Put another way, the price of gold remains relatively stable over time.

Had the alchemists found an artificial way of creating gold, they would have killed its value. Its flow would have increased rapidly, making its existing stockpile less critical to its price. Successful alchemy would have defeated its own purpose. If there had been a cheap way to make new gold, the metal wouldn't have remained scarce for very long. Thus, its price would have decreased over time. But, it would have made the individual alchemist very rich in the process.

Central Banking is successful alchemy in this sense. The money-issuing institutions of the world have found a way to create new money with no cost. No mining is required. They are the alchemists of our era. The Central Banks' promise of stable prices is as absurd as the alchemists' promise of cheap gold. The whole point of a value-measurement tool, or a type of money, is in its costliness. It has to somehow connect to reality because of the subjective nature of value. Money created without cost is like fools' gold.[2] It enriches the issuer and his friends while everyone else pays for the whole ordeal. This is also known as the *Cantillon Effect*. An effect named after the man who first noticed it, Richard Cantillon. The further away you are from a money printer, the more you pay for the counterfeiting.

---

[2] "Fool's gold" is another word for the mineral pyrite, or iron pyrite, an iron sulfide with the chemical formula FeS_2 — Iron disulfide. Pyrite is the most abundant sulfide mineral in nature. Pyrite's metallic luster and pale brass-yellow hue give it a superficial resemblance to gold, hence the well-known nickname of fool's gold. Like bitcoin cash to bitcoin, fool's gold is worth a fraction of the real thing.

Alchemy might seem absurd to a person with a basic understanding of chemistry. But it's even more ridiculous from a praxeological perspective. It defeats its own purpose. The alchemists should have been looking for the properties of gold, not gold itself. What if an alchemist had been able to replicate the monetary properties of gold instead? Our view of alchemy would have been very different. What if you could recreate the properties of gold? What if you could improve them? Would you then have stumbled upon a new element? Would we have to redefine chemistry?

Atoms make up gold and every other solid, fluid, and gas in the periodic table. Protons, electrons, and neutrons make up the atoms. If we zoom in even further, we enter the strange realm of quantum physics. Here, everything is probabilistic. Elementary, or fundamental, particles, make up the protons and the neutrons. The electrons are fundamental particles themselves. These particles are made up of nothing but pure information, it seems. They have no substructure. The information about the particle is the particle in essence. If we zoom in deep enough, everything is information. Elementary particles pop into our world every now and then and form elements. But the underlying spacetime field that everything stems from is a different beast altogether.

Here, there's nothing but information. At this level, things don't behave the same way as what we can observe at larger scales. In the quantum realm, particles behave probabilistically and have extraordinary properties. They can be *entangled*, influencing one another at vast distances. They can *spin* more than 360 degrees per rotation. All kinds of weird stuff. Science has no definite answer to why these fundamental particles behave the way they do. There are many different theories and interpretations. But let us focus on the information itself for now.

Regardless of how the universe really works, there's an informational layer at its core. Everything is made up of information. The smallest unit of space we know of is the Planck area. These areas are so small that they can only contain one unit of entropy, a single bit. The Planck length is expected to be the shortest measurable distance since any attempt to investigate the possible existence of shorter distances by performing higher-energy collisions would inevitably result in black hole production. That sounds like a horrible idea, don't you think? So for the sake of argument, let's just imagine that these Planck areas are the "pixels" of the universe. Pixels that consist of bits. A bit is the smallest unit of information. It expresses one out of two states. One or zero. On or off. True or false. Yin or Yang. The Planck area contains a qubit before its condition is measured. A qubit is both states at once. Both a one and a zero, both true and false. That is until an observer measures its current form. When this happens, the qubit collapses into one of these two states. Which state it will collapse into is impossible to know. But if you zoom out, there's a higher probability of it collapsing into one of the states rather than the other. In other words, the reality we live in is probabilistic at its core. No observer could ever calculate or measure the exact location of all particles in this universe. The map can never be the territory, but only a model of it. Uncertainty is always present. This is not a bad thing, though. If there was no uncertainty, everything would be predetermined. Free will couldn't exist.

Put another way, life would be a movie rather than a computer game if the universe was deterministic. You wouldn't be able to interact with anything. So at its core, everything is information, and so are you. Luckily for us humans, islands of certainty dot the vast ocean of uncertainty around us. Islands like the elements that make up physical matter. We interact with these physical objects by attaching a value to them. If we find an apple in nature, we may choose to eat it, thereby nourishing ourselves. We may also choose to ignore the apple for some reason, like if we're full and don't feel the need to eat at that moment. We may also choose to ignore it if we own an apple tree, in which case one extra apple would be of little use to us. This is known as the law of diminishing marginal utility. It states that the marginal utility derived from each extra unit of an economic good always declines. This is why scarcity is so essential to value judgments. We all attach different values to all the objects we encounter in life. These values always differ from person to person and occasion to occasion. There is no such thing as "equal value." It is always dynamic. A chair, for instance, may be regarded as a helpful tool to one person but be an obstacle to another. We figure out how others value all things by participating in trade. The market gives us information about other people's value judgment through prices. Through prices, the market reveals what others value.

Prices are a reflection of the wants and needs of other people. If you tamper with the properties of money, you reduce the functionality of all price signals. Central banks do this to government-issued currencies all the time. These have an ever-increasing supply. Thus, the value of each unit of a government-issued currency is constantly decreasing. The market discovers stability in an otherwise uncertain world. But its ability to do so depends on the predictability of the money issuance rate. Money is the tool that we use to find stability in markets. It functions as a ruler that tells market participants how to best spend their time and resources. What means to seek out to reach their desired ends. Now try to imagine a way to measure subjective value judgments objectively. Presume that the sum of every personal value judgment could be expressed through an element on the periodic table. What properties would such an element need to have? To find out, we first need to understand what makes something money. Money has seven essential characteristics — durability, portability, divisibility, uniformity, limited supply, and acceptability.

So first and foremost, such an element would have to be stable. An unstable isotope wouldn't suffice. Resistance to change is crucial for an element aspiring to function as a store of value. Moreover, our new element would have to be portable and divisible. Portability and divisibility are two sides of the same coin (pun intended). This implies that our imaginary addition to the periodic table would need to weigh as little as possible. It would also have to be uniform or fungible.

Furthermore, it must have a limited supply; the total amount of the element would have to be finite. If we could find such an element, people would accept it as payment for goods and services. It would live up to all the criteria needed to become a type of money. Because gold is one of the two known stable, non-radioactive, non-toxic, mononucleic noble metals, it satisfies the essential characteristics of money. The fact that the free market discovered gold as an excellent form of money is quite remarkable. People participating in the free market 5000 years ago knew nothing about chemistry. Neither were they aware of praxeology or even the number zero. Let alone quantum mechanics and theories about a possible multiverse. Yet, the market chose a truthful form of money. The free market somehow knew what money had to be and do. Gold has a downside, though — its weight. Despite its excellent monetary properties, it is not that easy to transport. Gold is, at its core, nothing but a dumb shiny rock, but dumb nonetheless. Too heavy to transport easily.

In the past, when people used gold for day-to-day transactions, its weight had a specific purpose. When you dropped a gold coin on the floor, it made a very distinct sound. As it did, you instantly knew that the coin was made out of the real deal. Hence the term *sound money.* Dropping a token to the floor was the common man's means of verifying its gold content. This was useful for a long time, but we now live in the information era. A type of money suited for our day and age would have to be a lot easier to move around than a dumb rock. Dumb rocks get hoarded and stockpiled in vaults by supervillains. We need something more flexible. So why not try to imagine a new element altogether?

What exactly would we be looking for if we did? Something durable, portable, divisible, and fungible with a limited supply. What would such an element look like? What chemical properties would it have? Well, its optimal atomic weight would be zero. The lighter the atom, the easier it becomes to move it around. Where would an element with no mass end up in the periodic table? Well, no weight means no protons or neutrons. This means that our imaginary chemical element would have the atomic number zero. This would place it in the upper left corner of the periodic table. A new starting point. A new origo. Point zero.

The first evidence of the number zero is from the Sumerian culture in Mesopotamia, some 5,000 years ago. Around the same time as gold was first used as money. The discovery of the number zero changed mathematics forever. It provided mathematicians with a tool to discover all sorts of other mathematics. Including, but not limited to, the mathematics of infinity, which is the opposite of zero in a way. The discovery of element zero might be even more profound. In some versions of the periodic table, you find more information about the elements than just their molecular weight. Information about an element's electronegativity and ionization energy, for instance. Our weightless substance would have to be able to both attract and bind electrical power. If it couldn't, it would hardly be an element at all. Something without mass nor energy would have no connection to reality at all. Our substance would also have to be robust. In other words, it would have to take a considerable amount of energy to destroy it. This electrical connection would be the only thing making our element "real." It cannot consist of protons and neutrons since these would give it mass. It will need to be weightless if it is to be sent over the internet. But an atom without mass wouldn't have a position in physical space either. So how could we detect an element that only "exists" because of a connection to energy?

We would have to find a pure, abstract expression of a specific amount of energy expended. Enter the SHA-256 hashing algorithm and the difficulty adjustment algorithm. Maybe we can find a solution if we approach the problem of "discovering" this element by reverse engineering it. A proof of energy expended to prove the existence of a unit of the element could be enough. A hash of a bitcoin block beginning with a predetermined number of zeroes is proof of exactly that. The validity of a bitcoin block is easy to verify since all you have to do is look at a number. Thus, finding a specific hash makes it easy to calculate the amount of energy expended searching for it. In other words, it would be tough to fake a hash of a bitcoin block. It would be almost impossible since it would be more costly to "fake it" than to actually make it. So, through Proof-of-Work, we may accomplish what we set out to do.

We set out to reverse engineer chemistry, to become true alchemists. No small task. A person finding one of these hashes would be the legitimate first owner of that particular unit of element x. The ethics of natural law teaches us this: finders keepers. In fact, there would be no difference between knowing about it and owning it. The person finding it would be its owner, regardless of others' opinions about ownership. It would be controlled by whomever finds it. The information about the element would be the element. We've already established that it couldn't exist in the physical realm. It would have to be pure information in the literal sense of the word. Bitcoin is that information. Satoshi Nakamoto stumbled upon a new element, element zero, by releasing the bitcoin code. Whoever is behind the pseudonym didn't invent bitcoin. They discovered it.

So there now exists an element made up of pure information. An asset that only exists in the informational realm. A resource that one can beam across the internet at the speed of light. Held in the brains of its owners and exchanged by communication alone. An element that changes our relationship with information. Having more information about a particular thing than others has always been valuable. Knowledge is, at its core, the resolution of uncertainty. Knowing an answer to a simple yes- or no question can make all the difference. A single bit can represent the answer to a specific question like "Is the game rigged to player A's advantage?". If you know the answer to this one-bit question, a big reward could await you after a well-placed bet. Information like this has indirect value, but value nonetheless. The more society aggregates around communication, the more valuable information becomes. Communication is peaceful interaction. Violence is what humans resort to when communication fails. This is why having correct information is so crucial.

With the introduction of bitcoin, information itself became valuable. Information now has a literal value. This is an abstract concept, and it's challenging to discern its implications. Holding the private keys to a specific bitcoin address is owning bitcoin. In bitcoin, there is no difference between knowing and owning. You have to convert information with an indirect value into something tangible before you can trade it for something else. The bet itself can buy you nothing, but the winnings can. In bitcoin, the information representing the asset is the asset. There's no clear distinction between information about bitcoin and bitcoin itself. When information is ownership, money becomes a language in the true sense of the word. It will put all the free speech laws of the world to the test. You can now claim ownership by communicating a string of numbers. Or by memorizing twenty-four words. The lines between knowing and owning are now forever blurred. The pen is now mightier than the sword, not only in a metaphorical sense but also in a literal one. The dynamics of violence are forever changed.

An element without mass is an incredible discovery. When you think about it, it's the solution to many societal problems. Whatever's wrong with how humans interact with the environment is one of those problems. The deflationary nature of bitcoin gives everyone an incentive to save rather than spend. It is the literal key to a future without overconsumption. An era in which physical stuff is as abundant as now but not as desirable to humans.

On a side note, as many of you know, energy and mass are two sides of the same coin. E equals mc squared. If you add up all the energy consumed since bitcoin's inception and divide it by 21 million, you get about 37 GigaJoules. That's the equivalent of 0.415 micrograms per bitcoin. In other words, bitcoins cost around 90 billion dollars per kilo right now.

3

OWNERSHIP

*I*NTELLECTUAL PROPERTY is a term that refers to a work or invention resulting from creativity. A manuscript or a design, for instance, to which one has rights. Things that one may attach a patent, copyright, or trademark to. The invention of the mp3 turned that definition on its head. Audio files were suddenly shareable among internet users because they had become small. A domino had fallen over that would soon make the entire record industry obsolete. And not only the record industry but the whole entertainment industry. Any computer file could now be shared with anyone on Earth over the internet for free. The information age had begun, and the industrial era was about to end. Now, a quarter of a century later, big data rules the world. "Intellectual property" is almost a thing of the past, even though archaic copyright laws still stand. Nowadays, we pay for access to music, movies, books, and articles in other ways. Either by subscribing to media services or by giving away information about ourselves. Advertising companies then buy this information to bombard us with ads for things they believe we're likely to buy.

As described in the previous chapter, a purely informational asset now exists. A way to convert energy into a yardstick for measuring the value of human time. Something abstract that you can claim ownership of by knowing about it. Something that will change the definition of intellectual property. Chances are that it might even put the word "ownership" itself to the test. For what is ownership, if not the ability to resist confiscation? Every material thing is confiscatable. Every mansion, gold bar, and painting is at risk of being stolen at all times. If you live in a peaceful country, this risk might be low, but it's a risk nonetheless. Does this mean that you can't really own physical stuff? Well, if we use this definition of ownership, it does.

From this point of view, all you can own is your time and your bitcoin. Bitcoin has completely flipped the board when it comes to defining property. When knowing and owning are conflated, the dynamics of violence change. A lot. The world's most ownable and valuable good is now a non-confiscatable, abstract number. When you cannot know how much a person owns, and when you can't take it by force, there's just no way of enriching yourself other than by providing something of value to your fellow man. To comprehend all aspects of what this implies boggles the mind. It compels us to rethink everything about how we organize ourselves. In this sense, we are cave trolls trying to imagine Boston Dynamics. Bitcoin is not a threat to civilized society but rather the beginning of it.

Now, what does all this mean for the economic models of the internet? Advertisements finance the internet as we know it today. All different media platforms compete for our attention. We're constantly spoon-fed with imaginary titbits that trick the reward mechanisms in our brains. Every new notification or bunch of points in a game triggers a dopamine release in our heads. We're nudged into clicking on ads and suspicious links all the time. We're led to believe that our apps are free, but they're not. There is no free lunch, and there never was. We're paying for stuff with our attention and our time. The more information we feed into the algorithms, the easier it becomes to manipulate us. Artificial intelligence finds connections between our past and future behavior. Patterns that we don't even know ourselves. The algorithms that figure us out get exponentially better over time, and we cannot keep up with them. But is this phenomenon limited to social media and gaming? Far from it. The ultimate behavior manipulation scheme ever invented is money printing. Those who have the power to print money can make whole societies submit to their wants and desires. Imagine that you are in charge of issuing new dollars for the Federal Reserve Bank of America for a second. How do you go about it? What does the actual process look like? Most new dollars aren't even printed today but mere entries in a database. New dollars are made in three simple steps. First, you log into the money-making portal, then you put your cursor at the end of a number in an account on the desired bank ledger. After that, you add a desired amount of zeroes to this number. Then you press "Enter" on the keyboard. Conjuring new dollars into existence out of thin air takes less effort than writing the word "dollar." In other words, the word "dollar" is costlier to produce than an actual dollar. An mp3-file locks up a couple of megabytes of data on a hard drive, but creating new dollars is of almost no cost whatsoever. Producing currency has never been cheaper. If money wasn't inexpensive to produce, prices couldn't have remained stable for very long. And price stability is absolutely crucial to the consumer economy we live in today. This is absolutely necessary for the fiat monetary system to function at all.

All other things that have been on this production price reduction path have had one thing in common. They're incredibly cheap now. Movies, music, and books are almost free today compared to what they used to cost. Products made up of information, like songs, books, and even movies, are nearly infinitely cheap to produce. Most people don't realize that the same thing is happening to every physical good in the world. The actual production cost of everything money can buy is approaching zero and doing so fast, including transportation of these goods. But we're led to believe that prices are going up every year. Since money is the cheapest thing to produce, prices will continue to rise. When you can conjure currency into being out of thin air, prices will go up. Faster and faster. The only workable defense against this is bitcoin. As long as there's a demand for bitcoin, the cost of producing new ones will go up in proportion to this demand. This is the genius of the difficulty adjustment algorithm. Every 2016th block (or about once a fortnight), the difficulty rate of finding the following 2016 blocks is recalibrated. The average time needed for the network to find the next block in the bitcoin blockchain is always around ten minutes.

Since the beginning of 2020, the M2 money supply of US dollars has gone up by more than 20%. About 7,000,000,000,000 dollars were printed in 2021. That's about 222,000 dollars per second. In the meantime, a new bitcoin was created about every 96th second. 222,000 times 96 is around 21 million. So, in 2021, about 21 million dollars were created per every new bitcoin. To call this poetic would be an understatement, to say the least. Sooner or later, all this money printing will affect the dollar's purchasing power. And bitcoin's purchasing power, for that matter. Also, during 2020 all US citizens received "free" stimulus checks on several occasions. Most people took the bait. Not realizing what a "free" stimulus check really is.

Almost all countries took similar measures to lessen the financial impact of the virus. Nearly all of these measures have increased people's dependency on the state. They're transforming able-bodied workers into couch potato voting cattle. Those who still have a job work harder and harder every year to keep up with the inflation. The system is unstable by design, but we're led to believe that it's not.

Beware of anything advertised as free. There's no such thing as a free lunch. Those who promote products as "free" want to make you dependent like you owe them for their "generosity." When your livelihood depends on handouts from those in power, you become valuable to them because you're unlikely to vote against them in the next election. It is hard for a man to understand something when his salary depends on him not understanding it. You are worth more to politicians as a vote-generating machine than you are as an actual productive citizen. The dollar is a shitcoin. So is the Euro, the Yuan, and everything else that isn't bitcoin. They're all pyramid schemes designed to deprive you of your time. If it's free, it's not money. It's a tool for controlling you in one way or another. Your attention is valuable, your labor is valuable, and your time is valuable. More valuable than you think. Don't give it away for free.

Monetary inflation is mass time-theft. It's a bottomless void. The US dollar is still the world's reserve currency, and the world prices oil in US dollars per barrel. When the Fed decides to conjure new dollars into existence, all products made from oil get more expensive. This includes everything made from plastics, which damn near all consumer goods are. When the purchasing power of the dollar drops, we all pay. Because of this, the currency spigot of the Federal Reserve is the most powerful one on Earth. Americans have a head start compared to everyone else. Since the dollar is so dominant, the US can exchange dollars for almost everything else. They can print little pieces of paper and trade them for any other good or service they want. Planetary-scale mass time-theft financed the American stimulus checks. It also paid for the war in Iraq and the war in Afghanistan. We all paid for it all, whether we were aware of it or not. Nothing the government does is free. There's no free social media platform either. They all come at a price, though it can be hard to realize who's paying for what. We live in an era where Keynesian economic thinking is everywhere. The central claim of this theory is that government spending is always a good thing. No wonder governments like it.

Because of this, interventionism is the norm, leaving no economy sound. Every economy is unsound, corrupt, and untruthful. The bad guys won. The people who have no moral quarrels about stealing. They won everywhere. Big finance plays by its own rules, and central banks keep interest rates low by artificial means. This benefits the largest companies in the world and not many others. It is getting worse over time, and it wouldn't have been possible without fiat currency. Inflation is increasing the prices of everything forever. Actual production and transportation costs are heading towards zero in an efficient system. Inflation is a force in the opposite direction. It has to be to keep prices "stable." Luckily, we have bitcoin. We're the rebels. The status quo is the galactic empire. Bitcoin is the photon torpedo fired at the Death Star's thermal exhaust port.

Digital products have always been free to copy. Still, software companies find ways to charge us for them. Either by subscription fees, ads or by collecting data about us. The internet should have changed everything, and in many ways, it did. But the companies that run the show today still operate under broken rules. Rules from an outdated economic paradigm. Every technology is deflationary by nature. Every innovation saves someone time, somewhere. As our tools get better, we produce more with less effort. All prices should reflect this. They should be going down. Instead, a tiny elite forces us to give up a considerable chunk of our time to pay for their excessive expenses. It's time to take matters into our own hands, and the tools we need for doing that are at our disposal already. If the money you're using gets devalued over time, it doesn't matter how diversified your portfolio is. If your fuel tank is leaking, it doesn't matter how good your fuel is. Inflation is a bit like a hole in a fuel tank. As time passes, that hole will grow larger.

There's no way of stopping the bust part of the boom-bust cycle that inflation always leads to. The policymakers can only postpone and enlarge the problem by printing even more money. Doing so is, in fact, the only option they have. All they can do is kick the can down the road. Or rather, roll the snowball down the hill. Sooner or later, economies will crash. The more they postpone this crash, the more severe the consequences. Provided enough time, we all have hyperinflation to look forward to. Inflation is a vector. That vector is a derivative of the money supply curve.

The angle of this vector gets steeper over time. At some point, all fiat currencies end up hyperinflating. There is no other way. The only way out of hyperinflation is through its polar opposite, hyperbitcoinization. It begins with you and me and when we start demanding compensation in bitcoin. Not when we start spending bitcoin, but when we start earning them. We're the ones that need to escape manipulation. Take a leap of faith. Faith in mathematics and game theory. The only belief required is that people will act in their own self-interest. A leap of reason, if you will.

On-chain bitcoins are anything but free. Sourcing and setting up a mining rig is expensive. It's hard to buy them without paying more than the market price. The electricity needed for mining is very costly too. The network itself has an in-built fee system for prioritizing transactions. But there's more to it. Exchanges have their own fees and so do bitcoin ATMs. Many services force you to give up some personal information. Bitcoin gains are taxable events in most countries. On top of this, bitcoin's price goes up and down a lot. You have to consider this volatility when you decide to buy bitcoin. You have to be mentally prepared to hold on to them for a long time. Few realize that this costliness is a good thing, though. All the extra costs involved are a testament to the immense value of the network. Bitcoins are expensive to produce, costly to store, and not always cheap to trade on-chain. Being reckless with your bitcoins can be an expensive lesson in personal responsibility. In other words, ignorance is costly in bitcoin. Bitcoin is the cheapest monetary network to use by far when appropriately used. In this regard, bitcoin is in stark contrast to fiat currency, as fiat economic systems reward ignorance. At least, that's what the central banksters want you to believe. In reality, ignorance is always expensive.

Nowadays, you can use bitcoin's second layer, the Lightning Network, for day-to-day payments. You can use the base layer for more critical transactions, and the network fees are still very cheap. Especially in comparison to what a settlement transaction in gold will cost you. If you're not paying for a traditional financial service, chances are that someone is taking advantage of you. You might not be the client at all, but the product. Whenever you use a bank-issued credit- or debit card, your transaction is recorded in a database. Your actions always end up in a spreadsheet somewhere. You're paying for everything twice. Once with your money and once with information about your spending habits. You already have a *social credit score*, whether you like it or not. Your government loves this kind of information. The Chinese government is already using data like this to control their population. The Chinese people's social credit score determines the extent of their freedoms. It is a tool for mass obedience. All nations are en route to more surveillance and fewer freedoms. A very Orwellian future awaits us if we don't address these problems. Governments certainly won't solve them. Neither will banks nor any other big institution. We have to address them ourselves.

The great John Cleese once described the people of the town that he grew up in, Weston-super-Mare, as "people who yearned to get safely into their coffins without ever having been seriously embarrassed." This fitting description of your average dullard citizen can serve as a reminder to us all. A reminder that most people are content with being docile sheep and a reminder that life is precious. Life is not a rehearsal. The sooner you realize this, the sooner you want to reclaim your sovereignty. The dullards are everywhere, and they will get used by totalitarians. If you want to avoid waking up in a communist dictatorship one day, be more like Cleese and less like the people he grew up around. Embrace and enjoy your life. It's the only one you've got.

The internet can never be a true representation of reality. An accurate computer simulation of reality would have to be reality itself. In other words, maps are always flawed. A completely accurate map of something would have to be an exact copy of that something. The map is, by definition, not the territory. The blueprint is not the product. Information about reality is not reality. Money is information about the real world. Information about who owes what to whom. Information about people's wants, needs, and means. The monetary bill was first introduced to the world as a receipt for gold stored in a vault. Gold was a physical token. This receipt contained data about that token written on a piece of paper. The internet deals exclusively with information, and the web is made up of nothing but data. It is an informational realm. Thus, the only way to track who owes what to whom on the internet is by using a ledger. A ledger, a list, or a spreadsheet, usually requires someone in charge of its entries. A trusted third party.

The goldsmiths of the past could, and certainly did, manipulate their ledgers. They could lend out more receipts for gold than they actually stored in their vaults. This type of ledger manipulation is even easier for the keeper of a ledger on the internet. Physical tokens are much harder to manipulate than digital ones. If someone gives you an apple as payment for something, you can verify the "realness" of that apple by taking a bite of it. Physical tokens of value come with a different set of problems. Gold has been a popular form of money for around five thousand years. But gold is relatively easy to confiscate due to its physical nature. Throughout the ages, governments everywhere have confiscated almost all of the world's gold. Because of this, the lion's share of the gold resides in the vaults of the world's central banks. Institutions that lend out way more receipts for this gold than they should. Gold required centralization and a paper currency built on top. When banks tried to leverage that too far, and there was a market panic, people came to get their gold only to find there wasn't enough gold in the vaults. In other words, there was a bank run. Bank runs force the central bank and government to seize the gold and reprice it to avoid societal collapse and civil war. Leverage leads to instability which leads to the "need" for intervention. The problem the central banks claim to "fix" is created by the system itself since the smaller banks are allowed to lend out more than they have in their vaults.

Both physical and informational representations of value come with a set of problems. Physical tokens are not convenient as money. Digital ledgers require trusted third parties. The physical realm is suitable for storing value through time. The informational domain is more ideal for sending value through space. Neither is good at both. The bitcoin blockchain is a ledger that does not require third-party interference. It is a type of money that can send value through time and space. A loss-free energy network that anyone on Earth can participate in.

Bitcoin creates information that affects physical reality through its users. The miner who finds the next block gets the reward. Like pirates of the Caribbean, miners look for treasure using a compass. For the Bitcoin miner, this compass is a computer or a bunch of computers, powered by electricity. A real-world resource that can't be faked. The treasure the miner finds is a treasure map. In bitcoin, the map is the treasure. If you find the map, you get the reward. You cannot acquire this map without looking for it. The more you look, the greater the chances that you'll find it. And you can only look for it by firing up more computers. You create computing power by sacrificing things from physical reality. Energy and time. This computing power is the engine that spawns the next bitcoin block into existence. A gold miner finds gold by using gold mining equipment. A bitcoin miner finds bitcoin using bitcoin mining equipment. Bitcoin miners dig for element zero on the periodic table. The element without mass. The informational element. Only when they can prove that they've found it they actually have. In bitcoin, the proof of the element's existence is the element itself. All mining operations require time, effort, and energy. Bitcoin has an in-built difficulty adjustment algorithm to keep the block time interval constant. A fascinating, elegant feature of how bitcoin works. By adjusting how hard the next bitcoin is to find once every 2016th block, bitcoin becomes its own clock. It defines its own time. The algorithm ensures that it always takes around ten minutes for the network to find the next block. The successive block's hash is always lower than the current difficulty. This is one of the criteria in the very definition of a valid block. The proof of its existence is what spawns it into being. This makes bitcoin a Perpetuum Mobile as long as there are miners around. Tick tock, next block. It works because Proof-of-Work requires energy. You cannot fake it. There are no shortcuts. That's what Proof-of-Work means. An irrefutable proof that the required effort was actually put in. You're going to have to spend energy from the physical realm to find the next block. There's no way around this. In bitcoin, the map is the territory. This is one of the most mind-blowing aspects of it. It is a history book not written by a subjective winner but by truthfulness itself. Since you can verify that the ledger is correct, it is by far the most accurate record of history ever known to man. You can verify that it's truthful by looking at some zeros in front of a number. We're building the bitcoin economy upon a base layer of pure truthfulness. Every transaction on the ledger actually happened. It is a truth machine, in the literal sense of the word.

If our societies aren't truthful, we become more suspicious of them. This leads us to adopt a higher time preference. There's a strong correlation between truthfulness and time preference. The more robust society is, the more we can rely on its mechanisms and the more long-term thinkers we can afford to be. Long-term thinking is a luxury for those who can afford it. Few today can, since the rules of every nation change over time. New laws are written, and new rules come into play every day. This phenomenon alone forces us to adopt a higher time preference. To think more short-term. The fear of losing what we have makes us more irrational and egoistic. When we first lay our hands on something that cannot be taken away from us, we can allow ourselves to be less self-centered. Less fearful. When we're less afraid, we can prioritize the well-being of ourselves and our families. What is the opposite of fear? It's love!

There's a strong connection here. Time preference is on a spectrum from high to low. But on that same spectrum is fear and love. Egoism and altruism. Contrary to what those in favor of social engineering want you to believe, having less money is more likely to make you more egoistic than having more. This is at least true for sound money. Bitcoin is a measurement of truthfulness, and it's correlated to how much we can allow ourselves to love and to what extent we can let love influence our decisions. The closer we are to the truth, the more loving and peaceful we become. The further we drift away from it, the more fearful and hostile we become. Beware of fear mongers that try to force love out of your life. Let go of your fear and your ego. Focus on finding the truth. Only then will you be set free.

4

ENERGY

I N physics, energy is the quantitative property that must be transferred to a body or physical system to work on it or heat it. The law of conservation of energy states that the total energy of an isolated system remains constant. In other words, it is said to be conserved over time. Energy is needed to make things happen. Without energy, the world would be a very dull place. If bitcoin is an element without mass, it consists of nothing but pure information. But a weightless element can also be described as an element of pure energy. As described earlier, the only thing giving a massless element a connection to reality is its ability to bind energy. Bitcoin is energy. It converts electricity into another, less specific kind of energy. A form of energy that humans haven't encountered before. We could call it monetary energy, but bitcoin is more than just money. Bitcoin is condensed time. A perfect reflection of the value of human time. In other words, a bridge between electrical energy and energy expressed through human effort. Scientists have searched for a unifying theory of everything for a long time. Quantum mechanics and Einstein's theory of relativity do not match. The very small and the very large seem to be governed by different natural laws. Through bitcoin, humanity may have stumbled upon another critical discovery. A connection between the physical and the neurological realm.

The laws of thermodynamics are deceptively simple to state but far-reaching in their consequences. The first law of thermodynamics is now applicable to the inner workings of the human mind. It asserts that if heat is recognized as a form of energy, then the total energy plus its surroundings is conserved. In other words, the universe's total energy remains constant. The second law may be formulated by observing that the entropy of isolated systems left to spontaneous evolution cannot decrease. They always arrive at a state of thermodynamic equilibrium where the entropy is highest at the given internal energy. An increase in the system's and its surroundings' combined entropy accounts for the irreversibility of natural processes, often referred to as the arrow of time. Bitcoin provides a way to quantify human valuations while respecting the laws of physics. At least to the maximum extent possible. By sacrificing electricity to find a specific number, bitcoin uses entropy to find order. In doing so, it converts electricity into a perfect representation of the value of human time. Thinking of bitcoin as energy has many benefits when talking to pre-coiners. First, it can be challenging to convince the average person that they need a new form of money. Convincing them that a new, digital form of energy now exists might be more manageable. You could even call it mathematical energy. Because what is bitcoin, if not the utilization of mathematics to express value? No political leader on Earth is "against energy." This new mathematical form of energy will play an essential part in power plant construction in the future.

Right now, the energy sector suffers from bad political optics. The energy sector provides a perfect example of how destructive politics can be. So what is going on here? Let's start from the beginning by dissecting the logic of environmentalism. Global temperature measurement trends show that the Earth is warming. A plethora of climate models shows that this is a terrible thing. This may be true to a greater or lesser extent, but the notion of danger itself has a dangerous side-effect. Because of a bias in our brains, we humans tend to overemphasize negative news. Both the media outlets and the politicians know this. They know that good news doesn't sell very well. They know that you need a cause to rally around to get the votes.

Environmentalism is one such cause. Since the seventies, "green" parties and political agendas have played a more prominent role in every country. Today, environmentalism is everywhere in politics. Environmentalists emphasize the need for renewable energy sources. New wind- and solar farms are being built in the EU, the US, and China. The advertised intention is to replace fossil fuels and nuclear energy as soon as possible. But there's a problem. Renewables aren't as reliable an energy source as nuclear power is. This means that as renewables take over, it becomes more challenging to plan ahead energy-wise. A catch 22 situation arises. For the energy grid to be sustainable, it needs to be reliable over long periods. Nuclear power is very reliable from a physics standpoint.

From a political perspective, however, it is not. In democratic societies, the whims of public opinion can have devastating effects on energy reliability. Because of this, nuclear power plants might not be a good idea in democracies. The initial investment to build a nuclear power plant is steep, and the plant needs to produce electricity for about fifty years to recover this initial cost. Although the investment makes sense from a physics standpoint, history has shown that the "will of the people" almost always changes over fifty years. In California and Northern Europe, we're seeing the problems with unplannable energy politics play out right now. These areas have steadily increased their dependence on renewable energy sources. This switch has led to an unreliable electricity supply and saddled its residents with high and fluctuating energy costs. Add to this that electric vehicles are becoming more and more popular. When people actually run out of electricity, bad things follow. It is not "good for the environment" by any stretch of the imagination. People with no access to reliable, reasonably priced energy sources quickly adopt a higher time preference. Simply stated, they prioritize short-term decisions. This is true for both the common man and the factory owner. Short-term decision-making is the problem. Energy use and solutions to environmental issues require an ability to plan. Environmentalist policies remove that ability by constantly pulling in the opposite direction.

All too often, those proclaiming that the end is nigh are the same people who put us all at risk. According to these people, the direr the cause, the more it justifies drastic means. In reality, specific ends can never justify any means. Every acting human being uses means to reach his own particular goals. Through the eyes of the individual actor, these means are always justified by their ends. If they weren't, the action wouldn't have taken place at all. Giving those in power more power to combat a specific issue is rarely a good idea. It almost always has the opposite effect of what effect it's intended to have. As people become more fearful of the future, they become more inclined to vote for more "control." Fear is critical to politicians since fear can justify all means and control in the frightened public's eyes. Wars are being waged against invisible enemies to keep the population fearful. Terror, drugs, poverty, climate change, viruses. Fighting a war against any of these phenomena is a fool's errand. The only thing such wars can lead to is more government control.

More false promises, more money printing, more problems, more fear. A vicious downward spiral emerges. More and more individual rights are given away in favor of causes supposedly of a greater good to society. People tend to forget that society is nothing but the individuals in it. This crucial fact is often lost somewhere along the path to totalitarianism. Society is you and me. Few fights would be left to fight without terrorists, junkies, poor people, climate change, and viruses. In such a world, politicians would serve no purpose. Therefore, it is not in their self-interest to ever solve a societal problem. Only to wage a perpetual war against it. You're the terrorist they want you to be afraid of. You're the junkie they wish to imprison. You're the carbon they wish to reduce and the virus they hope to contain. You're the poor person that won't vote against his own livelihood, which only they can provide. To put it another way, you're the victim in need of a savior. Assigning a politician to solve a societal problem is a bit like hiring a convicted pedophile to babysit your kids.

The European Central Bank President Christine Lagarde called for the global regulation of cryptocurrencies in January of 2021. "If there is an escape, that escape will be used," she said. The European Central Bank wants a regulatory framework for bitcoin. Mrs. Lagarde and her institution ought to have figured out that she can't do much about it at this point. Thinking that anyone can is one of the most common misconceptions about bitcoin. That someone somewhere could "do something" about it. No one can do anything about bitcoin. Not Christine Lagarde, not the World Economic Forum, not the International Monetary Fund, and not the United Nations. Nor could any politician, for that matter. No one is in charge of bitcoin, and there's nothing anyone can do about its existence. These people ought to be a little more humble in their approach. A local ban on bitcoin will only make the users in that jurisdiction use bitcoin more cleverly and privately. Or move to a more freedom-friendly part of the world.

The more freedom-friendly the place, the more that place will thrive from having a lot of bitcoiners there. A restriction on electricity use might force the local miner to close his business. Simultaneously, it will make mining more profitable for others in bitcoin-friendly jurisdictions. This effect gives nation-states an incentive to be more bitcoin-friendly. Satoshi designed bitcoin to thrive in adversarial conditions so that attacks against it would only fortify its immune system. This immune system is made up of individual nodes all around the world. It ensures that no more than 21 million bitcoins will ever be available. Absolute mathematical scarcity. Unforgeable production costliness of a monetary good. Humanity has never had that before. Nation-states and central banking have been around for eons, but this absolute mathematical scarcity is an entirely new phenomenon.

A central bank is a centralized institution that issues a nation-state's money. The new money is then given to said nation's government in exchange for government bonds. Bonds are a promise from the government to pay back the loan at an unknown point in the future. However, that money is owed back with interest. So for every $1 created, more than $1 is demanded to be returned. But because of the interest on the loan, there's never enough fiat money in circulation to pay it back. Fundamentally, the system runs on debt. There must always be more debt than capital in a fiat monetary system. This is always the case when banks conjure fiat money into existence. Fiat money is debt. The prevailing economic theories behind the mechanics of money states that this is a good thing. Perpetual debt keeps people incentivized to spend their money.

Fiat economists believe spending to be a good thing since every trade produces a new good or service. And there's no limit to how many times you can spend a 100 Euro bill, right? Well, spending can be good for an economy, but it doesn't have to be. An investment in something that can produce value in the future is a good thing. Wasteful consumption, for consumption's sake, is not. It's an illusion of economic progress rather than actual economic improvement. The damage central banking has done to the world is immeasurable. And every country in the whole world still believes its untruthful promises.

What we live in today is a world based on consumerism. Wasteful spending at the expense of future generations. No wonder we have environmental problems. Production and transportation costs are lower than ever. The price vectors all point in the same direction. Zero marginal costs. But fiat money already has a zero marginal cost, and today's high prices are artificial. The only thing that can give you a hint of how cheap everything has become is bitcoin. Its ever-increasing purchasing power is a testament to how fooled we've been. Denominated in bitcoin, all prices fall, as they should. The production of more junk is of almost no cost to the producers of that junk. It's costly to the consumer but not as expensive as not spending your money at all. Everything has an opportunity cost. There's always a choice. In a bitcoin-denominated world, we can all access the riches of the abundant future. Bitcoin reduces wastefulness and increases truthfulness. It emits freedom dioxide, expanding all of our freedom footprints.

All we have to do is alter our time horizon. With bitcoin, we can all get everything we want by saving money. It's that simple. But the most beautiful side-effect of the system is that we'll stop over-consuming. Bitcoin's dilution-proof technology ensures that everyone stays disincentivized to spend. No one wants to let go of a monetary good that goes up in value over time. Everyone will be more careful with their money. This is what the world needs and what everyone in it needs personally, too. But it's not the only way bitcoin can help the environment. Most of the criticisms about its energy use focus on the costliness of mining. But the critics are all missing the point. The energy cost for mining is what makes bitcoin work. The miners compete for a specific reward in a sum of new bitcoins every ten minutes. The more miners connected to the network, the more severe the competition becomes. The difficulty adjustment algorithm ensures this. Mining bitcoin gets more costly in energy terms as the total number of miners grows. But what is money, if not energy? Money provides humans with a tool for converting energy between different states. Your labor is a form of energy, as are the things you buy with the fruit it provides.

Furthermore, the cost of mining bitcoin is directly proportional to its value. The more demand there is for bitcoin, the more valuable it becomes. The higher its price, the more new miners will come online. The more miners that come online, the costlier the mining process. The pricier the mining process, the higher the price of the recently found coins. It's a positive feedback loop. Money condenses energy. Bitcoin is the first and only tool for converting electric energy directly into monetary energy. Now, what will this do to the energy market? First, miners will continually search for the cheapest energy sources available. They all operate under an ever-increasing incentive to cut their electricity costs. Renewable energy is the most affordable form of energy when it actually works. Right now, much of it doesn't. It exists because it's on life support. Without government subsidies, there would have been no wind turbines. Without the deliberate hampering of the nuclear power markets, renewables wouldn't exist.

You might think of this as a good argument for renewables, but try to envision what the world will look like a little further into the future. Renewable energy sources will never be sustainable unless they can be profitable. Sooner or later, you run out of other people's money. Bitcoin miners look for the real thing. This is already happening, by the way. Around 66% of the electricity required to power the bitcoin network comes from renewables right now. This figure is below 10% for all other electricity-intensive industries.

To bitcoin miners, there's no transportation cost to the electricity. Electricity itself is only transportable within a limited range from a power plant. But you can deploy a bitcoin mining rig anywhere. They don't even have to be close to a human settlement. The ideal location would be a hydroelectric plant by a waterfall in a cold country to cool the miners. The energy generated there wouldn't need traditional means of transportation. It wouldn't need a power grid at all. It wouldn't even need a lot of bandwidth. The plant owner could store the energy in bitcoin, making bitcoin a value battery. In this sense, bitcoin can serve as a suspension mechanism for renewable energy. Whenever a surplus of power exceeds what the electric grid can carry, the mining rigs absorb what would otherwise have been wasted. All that excess energy that is going to waste will be harnessed and utilized, helping secure dilution-proof money in the future. Energy companies will become bitcoin mining companies. And vice versa. The discovery of an element without mass will change the way humans think about energy. Monetary energy is now as much a tangible form of energy as kinetic, mechanical, gravitational, or electrical energy. Electricity itself is a very evanescent thing. When you want to save electricity or send it through time, you need a battery. Electrical batteries lose their charge all the time. The same holds true for when you try to send electricity through space. Bitcoin is by far the energy network with the most negligible energy loss through both space and time. As discussed earlier in this book, other types of money are suitable for one of the two, but never both. Gold and precious metals hold their value over time, and fiat currencies can easily be moved through space. Bitcoin is the first energy network that accomplishes both.

Robustness, in general, has to start from robustness in money. If we want our societies to be sustainable, we need them to be robust. Put another way, we don't want the rules to change too often. Democracy is slow to pivot because the bureaucracy intrinsic to the system makes it sticky. But it does change over time and hardly ever for the better. Democratic systems always tend to lean towards more bureaucracy, never less. This sort of makes them predictable, but the bureaucracy itself stifles innovation and makes it difficult for new actors to enter the market. Add a central bank to the mix, and the long-term consequences will be disastrous. Money-printing misallocates resources all the time and makes long-term thinking more difficult. Not only because it reduces the ability to save capital but also due to the increased unpredictability of the market. Bitcoin provides rules that cannot be changed by any human being. Rules without rulers. This is an absolutely critical prerequisite for sustainability. Without the ability to plan ahead, we would be truly doomed. Environmentalism is but a pointless political charade without it.

Claiming that bitcoin wastes energy is a testament to not only how little you know about bitcoin. But also to which extent you understand energy. Sacrificing, not wasting, energy would be a better term. But even that is a misrepresentation of what Proof-of-Work does. Bitcoin harnesses the energy and converts it. Whenever money is exchanged for goods or services, appreciation for people's labor is expressed through the transaction itself. Through trade, the energy stored in each money unit is converted into human work. If that money unit is part of an absolutely finite number of tokens, it can keep its energy forever. At least theoretically. If a government has access to a money printer, the energy stored gets diluted every time it's used. Paying for governments by diluting the value of money is a bit like draining a battery. Imagine leaving all the apps and gadgets on your phone running at all times. Think GPS, the flashlight, the speaker, Bluetooth, and WiFi. Your battery would drain pretty fast if you did. This is what the government's bureaucratic machine does to your nation's economy. Its "services" are always available, even when no one asks for them. Bitcoin is a far better financial battery. They are seldom spent on unwanted things since it's always more profitable to save them for more dire times.

The alchemists of old should have been looking for the properties of gold, not gold itself. Today's environmentalists ought to be looking for the properties of sustainability, not things that seem sustainable at first glance. If you want to help save the planet, you need to start by understanding what's wrong with it in the first place. You can't have sustainability in an unsustainable economic system. A band-aid will not cure cancer. Reducing the symptoms of a disease is not the same as finding a cure for it. Politicians are band-aid salesmen in a malignant economy. Also, they're the ones that caused the problems in the first place. Natural renewable energy is the cheapest form of energy available. Nuclear comes close. A liter of plutonium can provide about the same energy as five thousand barrels of oil. Alarmist politicians have screwed up all the price signals, though. And not only by imposing taxes on one form of energy and subsidizing another. They've destroyed all price signals by interfering in the free market. The alarmists are right about one thing, though. Perpetual growth is a delusional fairy tale. In a fiat currency world, it is a necessary delusion. Without ever more consumerism, fiat economies don't work. Therein lies the problem. You can't fix a broken system from within that system. It requires a solution from the outside. A black swan event. Bitcoin is the solution.

5

MORALITY

You came into existence when you were born. At least your consciousness did. You have no memory of "you" from before your birth, and neither does anyone else. So there's little reason to think that your existence is a continuation of the life of some other being. There's little reason to suspect that you're a reincarnated version of someone else. Therefore, most people don't believe this. Belief in a life after death is much more common than a belief in life before birth. This isn't so strange since the thought of an afterlife is a comforting one. After all, death is a scary thing. If it hadn't been, living beings would have been much more uncommon than they are now. But what does a belief in an afterlife do to our psyches?

Well, one could argue that such a belief dilutes the value of our time on this Earth. As described earlier, time is the scarcest of all resources. Thus, it is our most valuable possession. Life after death would diminish the value of your life here and now. Inflating the supply of alive-time after death doesn't make your life more valuable, but less. In this sense, belief in an afterlife is similar to faith in fiat money. An existential money printer, if you will. Neither the money printer nor an imaginary afterlife can create value from thin air. This is an illusion. What it can do, is fool people into believing that this or that arbitrary thing matters. To someone who wishes to control your actions, this is very convenient.

Your consciousness here and now, at this specific moment, is all you have. Alongside your senses, it is the only other tool you have for interacting with the world around you. It is also the only tool you have for detecting the world around you at all. It interprets the signals from your senses to make sense of the world at every single moment. One cannot even know to which extent our minds create reality itself. On a deep philosophical level, one cannot even know if other beings genuinely exist. As pointed out by the French philosopher René Descartes in the 17th century, "I think therefore I am." Descartes asserted that the very act of doubting one's own existence served as proof of the reality of one's own mind. There must be a thinking entity if thoughts are to exist at all. Even this statement assumes a bit too much, though. All you can know is that some thinking is going on somewhere.

Some entity somewhere is experiencing something. For a human being to use this knowledge in any practical sense, she needs to assume the existence of other minds as well. Your life would be far less enjoyable if you acted as if other beings were mere figments of your imagination. Imaginary or not, you will encounter other beings, and you're going to have to interact with them in some capacity. So you might as well proceed as if they were a part of reality and had conscious minds of their own. It helps to assume that they have no afterlife to look forward to either. If they did, chances are high that they wouldn't value their time here on Earth much. Without valuations, people wouldn't act. We don't see things the way they are. We see things the way we are. We constantly evaluate our deliberate actions before we choose to act. A value assessment precedes everything we do.

Your legacy is your real afterlife. What you leave for your children and grandchildren, including the children themselves. Your DNA lives on in them, and if your children are lucky, you will have built something for them during your life. Something that will live on. A fortune, a house, a book, an idea, a movie, a song. Anything that you created that will live on after you're gone. That's your real afterlife. This is the meaning of life in a way. If you leave this Earth in a little better state than when you entered it, you beat the game of life. Most fiat jobs do not impart a sense of meaning. Especially not since there's a big chance that what they pay you won't even be enough to pay off that mortgage of yours. Financial constraints hinder us from seeking out purposeful activities. There's no overarching meaning of life. But you can choose to fill each day with meaningful activities. To discover what's meaningful to you, lower your time preference. If you're running around in a hamster's wheel all day, you'll never find meaning. In this sense, fiat culture is a breeding ground for nihilism.

In our current fiat denominated world, everyone is running around every day chasing a dragon they'll never catch. Like heroin junkies, people run around pursuing pointless careers that won't bring them anything but addictive material cravings. Your fiat career will never lead you to a state of inner peace. You can only find that by lowering your time preference and looking inwards. Don't get fooled by the existential inflationists. Those that wish to steal your time and attention. Reclaim the driver's seat of your life. Start attaching value to the only thing you actually own — your time. No one can do this but you. Your family and friends find your time valuable. So does your employer, if you have one. Take the leap.

Humans do stuff because they value things. One must act to survive. Everything ever done by a human that wasn't a mere instinct had a value assigned to it by that individual human before it happened. A preceding value judgment is necessary for deliberate action to occur. "Is this worth doing?" You choose to do what you do by ordering these value judgments into hierarchies. At each moment, you value one action over another. Then, and only then, you act. I'm choosing to pen this sentence rather than go to the kitchen and make myself a sandwich right now. It's a deliberate choice. This sentence is more valuable to me than every sandwich in the world right now. Life is replete with micro decisions.

We assign value to our actions all the time, and we choose our focus based on our value hierarchies. You can make a case for interacting with other people as if they do the same. To maximize your experience with other human beings, you will need to trade with them. This might sound harsh, but only if you have a narrow definition of trading. Every voluntary action is a trade. Every time you choose to interact with another human being, you trade with them.

In most cases, you trade information. You give the other person a manifestation of your thoughts by using your vocal cords and mouth. Not to mention your body language. They use their ears and brains to convert the sounds you made into information about you and what you said. A spoken sentence from a person you can see contains a massive amount of data. It includes a lot about not only the words themselves but also about the person uttering them. That person's dialect can give you a hint about their past. If they speak fast, they might be in a hurry. What kind of language they use can give you a clue about how much they know about you. The point is that we exchange a plethora of valuable information every time we talk. Every time we interact, many different exchanges occur, whether we recognize it or not. There's no real difference between trading words and trading material stuff. After all, material things are nothing but information at their core. Both parties assume that the exchange will be somewhat beneficial to them in a trade. Lest they had, the transaction wouldn't have happened at all. This applies to exchanging a corporation for a hundred million dollars as much as it applies to a simple chat between two friends. The only time we interact with each other without trading is when we use violence or the threat of violence. Forceful interactions are, by definition, not voluntary.

Accepting this simple truth will provide you with an excellent moral lens through which you can view the world. A basic moral instinct that you might remember from playing around in your schoolyard. To act morally is to not harm others. To not use force against them or steal their stuff. Everyone knows this. But we often fail to recognize how some entities coerce us and steal from us all the time. Think about that schoolyard, for instance. Why were you there to begin with? Who put you there and why? Who built the school and why? How was it financed? During class, your teacher taught you math, English, and physics. But you were also taught "social sciences." They "taught" you about how "society works."

You were told about how taxes help us cooperate and share resources so that society can function. Chances are that they also told you about "everyone's equal value" and how unfair the market economy could be. You weren't supposed to ask how anything could be of equal value at all since valuations are subjective. You weren't supposed to question the legitimacy of the school's existence. Not to mention the legitimacy of the taxes that paid for it. You were not supposed to ask yourself how an institution that kidnapped you from your parents for eight hours every weekday came to be. The daylight robbery of taxes and inflation has been around for as long as nations have. A government has no other way of making money than to take it by force from its citizens, and all governments want to spend more than they actually have, just like most humans do. Whether it's a monarchy, a dictatorship, or a democratic country doesn't matter. Violent coercion is still the only way for a state apparatus to fund itself. The world is full of Prince Johns, and there are but a few Robin Hoods around to stop them.

When someone takes your stuff or your money, something peculiar happens. Your time preference changes. If you have nothing, your top priorities will be consuming food and finding shelter. In a survival state of mind, there's no room for long-term investments. A broke, homeless person is probably not thinking about business models. Such a person is much more likely to spend his day looking for food and shelter. The more capital you own, the more you can afford to plan ahead for the future. A person with fewer resources will focus on more primal wants and needs. This phenomenon is also known as having a higher time preference. When something is stolen from you, you must re-evaluate your long-term plans. To put it another way, your time preference must get higher. When you fall victim to crime, you start focusing more and more on immediate rewards.

When you're deprived of something, you focus less and less on things with a delayed gratification attached to them. If you're robbed by a simple thief, this change in time preference is temporary. The thief is not very likely to steal from the same person twice. You can take measures to prevent similar things from happening again. Also, people around you will probably think of you as the victim and the robber as the perpetrator. However, being robbed by a taxman or a central banker is different. You're probably being deprived of a certain amount of your wealth each month through taxation and inflation. If you don't pay, chances are high that you will suffer dire consequences. You might even end up in jail. Your peers are not likely to help you either since the lion's share of the population thinks taxes and inflation are natural things. People have been "educated" about how "society works" throughout their school years. They will not question the legitimacy of the government's actions. A monthly tax will force you to adopt a higher time preference throughout your life. There's very little you can do about it. It keeps you running in your hamster's wheel. Working for the system week in and week out throughout your entire life. People very seldom take the time to sit down and think about why this is so. Taxes and inflation have been around forever, it seems, and there's nothing we can do about them, right? Right?

Let us rewind to the notion of an afterlife. Belief in an afterlife is a great tool. Not for the person holding the belief, but for anyone who wishes to control them. Throughout recorded history, religion and power have been inexorably linked. Belief systems provide human leaders with motivational tools. The introduction of ceremonial burial was one such tool. With the introduction of the burial ritual came the promise of an afterlife. This tool enabled tribal leaders to start wars with other tribes. Despots could now trick their subjects with the promise of a better life after this one here on Earth. This gave them immense power since they could now rally armies to further their causes. It enabled them to form nation-states. Controlled territories with loyal citizens living in fear of the armed forces. Because of people's beliefs, the divine right of the ruler became a part of their operating system. For centuries, this was the basis of governance for almost all nations. The rulers were half-gods through the people's eyes, and their rule was not to be challenged.

Today, collective belief systems dupe populations into immoral behaviors through more sinister means. As mentioned before, when a person thinks he will live forever, he will tend to value his life here and now less. Without a time constraint, life approaches worthlessness fast. Interestingly, if you had an infinite amount of time, all bitcoins would be yours at some point. Bitcoin's cryptography isn't perfect. But it's good enough to have a high probability of outlasting the human race. Given infinity, though, you would break the cryptography and find every private key sooner or later. Remember, we're talking about infinity here. Infinity is a very long time.

In our day and age, a new belief system called democracy has replaced organized religions to a large extent. Democracy is a method of governance in which the people allegedly have their say in every decision. The idea of a better life after death is no longer people's primary motivator. The temporal promise of a better life here and now is. We're led to believe that if we vote for this or that party, we can change the world for the better. If we just keep using the money they issue, we can all become rich and prosperous. But our elected leaders all leave out a crucial fact. A popularity contest every four years doesn't make theft more ethical. A preceding election doesn't make the forceful acquisition of the fruits of someone else's labor more moral at all. We're supposed to forget our schoolyard moral code as soon as someone claims to act out "the will of the people."

Moreover, inflation functions as a substitute for the thought of an afterlife. Religious leaders diluted people's valuation of their lives through a promise. The promise of immortality. The leaders of today make an even worse promise. Guaranteed costless prosperity. The gift of a free lunch. Quantitative easing is one of the methods that they use to conjure up new money. Usually, it's done in the following way. The government begins by issuing a bond. A government bond is a paper stating that it will repay a certain amount at a certain point in the future. It then gives this bond to the central bank, giving the government new fiat currency units in return. Fresh money that the government has to pay back with a specific interest. But what is this promise that the government bond makes? It's a promise to continue to use the threat of violence to steal wealth from the citizens. This is the promise the government exchanges for a devaluation of its currency. A national currency it forces its population to use. It's a promise that the beatings will continue until morale improves. Paid for by the enslaved people themselves, twice. First, in an indirect way through the dilution of their purchasing power. Then by forcing them to pay taxes in a very straightforward way. Because of the obligation of the government bond, there's no way around these taxes. It's a perpetual downward spiral.

You might start to see a pattern. Here's what we've concluded so far. Your consciousness is born into this world. You know that it exists on some level since it thinks it does. Soon after you come into existence, you realize that, in this world, you'll need to act to survive. You start evaluating your options and act upon the ones you value the most. Acting includes interacting with other conscious beings. At some point, you also realize that using violence is dangerous. Doing things voluntarily not only feels better but produces better outcomes. Both for you and the person, or persons, you're interacting with. Acting implies choosing between a set of actions. You decide by arranging your wants and needs into a value hierarchy. To optimize the outcome of interactions we have with other people, we trade. We do so by acting as if the other party also had an inner value hierarchy, although we could never prove this to be true.

Trade is the voluntary exchange of information, especially if you consider quantum mechanics. Quantum mechanics has shown us that even physical matter is nothing but tiny bits of information. The fundamental particles that make up physical matter are information. When we measure them, they collapse into a binary state. True or false, one or zero, yin or yang. We all have a limited amount of time on this Earth. It has always been hard for us to assign a truthful value to this time. Leaders of early civilizations used the fear of death innate in all living beings to their advantage. They convinced other humans of the existence of an afterlife. Doing this diluted people's perceived value of their time. The same is being done today through inflation and the dilution of the purchasing power of your national currency. Mainly because money ought to be a representation of our limited time.

Monetary inflation has replaced existential inflation. And monetary inflation is arguably even worse because it's more direct. Money is supposed to represent time, after all. Inflation compromises time itself. But in 2008, an anonymous programmer released a paper that led to the discovery of a new element. An element with a fixed supply and without mass. A substance that exists only in the informational realm. A type of money that can represent the scarcity of human life. An asset that provides us with a way of proving to others that we own a specific part of a fixed number. An asset that you can store in your head. An investment that dies with you if you haven't passed it on before leaving this Earth. A perfect measurement tool for the value of human time. A tool to limit the profitability of violence and false promises. A connection between time, information, and morality.

The thought of a "higher power" or an unquestioned authority is always perilous, to say the least. So is the belief in an afterlife or that some entity can produce value by printing more money. To find meaning and morality in the short time we have, we need to rid ourselves of all appeals to authority. All of them. We need to question everything to have a shot at reclaiming the driver's seat of our lives. Only then can we find the meaning of our lives. We get to decide that meaning. We don't have to buy into whatever ideas the authorities shove down our throats. Only when we stop believing in false promises can we find our own individual purpose and meaning in life. We find our true selves by accepting life's boundaries and how precious it is to be alive. Having an open mind is essential, but it's worthless without intellectual honesty.

Many bitcoiners have likened the experience of understanding Bitcoin to a spiritual awakening. As your stack grows in purchasing power, you can afford to give yourself more time in the rabbit hole. You can spend more time finding your own personal purpose. Connecting with other so-called "bitcoin maximalists" is a great experience. Whether in real life or online, you can skip all formalities whenever you meet one. You can skip the social charade of talking about the weather. You know that the person you're talking to is already above a certain number of cognitive thresholds. This journey through hyperbitcoinization that we're all on is genuinely extraordinary.

All the great things it brings are easy to confuse with something supernatural. Words like "miracle" and "divine" seem less far-fetched than they used to. Buying into these new-age or neo-religious narratives is a dangerous path to be on. Remember how you found bitcoin in the first place and why you're convinced of its functionality. You're here because you're skeptical of narratives. Because you're a rigorous thinker. Because you don't trust. You verify. The temptation of coming to conclusions that aren't verifiable is always present. It is this very temptation that leads to belief in authority. Being a free thinker requires a tremendous amount of responsibility. If you want your mind to be free, you'll need to admit that you're the one in charge of your beliefs. If you let others dictate your ideas for you, you're not a free thinker. Intellectual honesty is critical. Be very careful when comparing bitcoin to a new religion.

Speaking of religion, let's examine the current dominant religion in the world for a moment. The belief that has taken the baton from the worship of supernatural entities. The religion of scientism. The ideas of the enlightenment might have propelled humanity forward in unprecedented ways, but they came with a side effect — a reverence for whatever "the scientists" say. Science is a systematic enterprise that builds and organizes knowledge. It attempts to find testable explanations and predictions about the universe. At least, that's what it's supposed to do. Scientists should question and test their theories over and over again. Only then can they lead humanity closer to understanding how the universe works.

Science may or may not be in line with a particular political agenda. Political agendas are not supposed to influence science. But all scientists are human beings. Humans are flawed creatures who act in the world because of incentives. We're conscious beings trying to rid ourselves of feelings of uneasiness. Our brains have cognitive biases. Scientists want to live fulfilling lives as much as the next guy. Their work may be fulfilling to a certain extent, but it is by no means the only thing that makes them act. A blind trust in whatever "the scientists say" is a dangerous thing. Blind trust is, in fact, the opposite of a scientific approach.

Today, many scientific endeavors receive funding from a very un-scientific entity — the government. This by no means means that all science is wrong. An unbiased scientist funded by the state can still make great discoveries, but state-funded science makes it harder to separate propaganda from the real deal. So does science financed by private entities, by the way. The state is a business. All businesses strive to increase their influence on the world. Wannabe intellectuals' homemade theories on social media make separating signals from noise even harder. Including whatever ideas yours truly happens to post. We all have to trust "the science" to a certain extent. No one has the time to test and verify every scientific theory. So how does one decide what to believe and what not to believe? Well, lo and behold, there's a correct scientific approach to this question too. A straightforward rule of thumb. Follow the money. This might sound harsh, but it makes perfect sense when you realize what money truly is. Actions speak louder than words as they represent people's true intentions. As Upton Sinclair once put it: "It is difficult to get a man to understand something when his salary depends on his not understanding it." Keeping this in mind, it is easy to see that the "harder" a science is, the more truthful it is. For instance, it is tough to cram a political agenda into mathematics. Some people do try, though. Mathematics has been called sexist and racist by those who understand it the least.

The natural sciences are "harder" than the social sciences by their very nature. The closer a science comes to pure logical deduction, the harder it becomes to falsify its claims. Mathematics comes very close to purely logical conclusions about reality. So does physics, even though it has entered a more philosophical realm as of late, especially after discovering quantum mechanics. "Gender studies" and "critical race theory" are about as far from a hard science as you can get. These "sciences" make assumptions about reality based on little but wishful thinking. They wouldn't exist, let alone propagate, if they didn't have a political agenda behind them.

The same is true for any "nutritional science" financed by the food industry. The vast amount of low-fat, gluten-free, "anti-inflammatory" products on the shelves of every supermarket are a testament to this. Take every branch of science directly connected to a profit motive with a large pinch of salt. Bearing this in mind, is there even such a thing as economic science? After all, every economic theory is bound to benefit one group more than another, right? Well, it doesn't have to. There is a scientific approach to economics. But it's not very popular. No single entity stands to benefit from its success. Thus it lacks funding from governments and large industries. I am, of course, referring to the science of human action. Praxeology. Praxeology is the study of economics from the perspective of the individual. The study of why human beings act with intention at all. It admits that a value judgment precedes every deliberate action a human takes. To the subjective world of valuations, praxeology is akin to what mathematics is to objective reality. Once you start viewing the world through the lenses of mathematics and praxeology, everything starts to make a lot more sense.

Proponents of religion as a necessary foundation for ethics often claim that science cannot derive an ought from an is. One could, however, argue that praxeology can. The science of human action doesn't make any moral judgments per se, but rather, it reveals the impact that violence, coercion, and theft have on our time preference. Being aware of other conscious beings' value hierarchies and their influence on these people's time preferences is a good start. You can easily see why voluntary interactions are almost always preferable to involuntary ones if you are aware of this. "When goods do not cross borders, soldiers will," French economist Frédéric Bastiat said in the early 19th century. This is true for more than just national borders. Every imaginary frame we put around each other can be broken forcefully or entered peacefully. We can only interact with each other in two primary ways. Voluntary or involuntary. With or without violence, or the threat thereof. Add a little game theory to the mix, and deriving an ought from an is becomes intuitive. Or rather, an ought not. Violent interactions have a higher risk of negatively impacting both parties' time preferences. Therefore, you ought not to steal, kill, or engage in other untruthful, violent activities.

These conclusions may be reached without any appeals to religion. No religious stories, metaphors, analogies, or commandments are necessary. They can, in fact, harm your understanding of ethics. "Sacred" texts often conflate moral guidelines with arbitrary things. Prayers and other rituals have little to no impact on reality. If you wish to waste as little of your precious time as possible, try to focus on how you can help your family and friends as much as possible. This will probably lead to a more fulfilling life than any cry for help from powers that may or may not exist.

"Pascal's wager" was a philosophical argument laid out by the seventeenth-century French philosopher, theologian, mathematician, and physicist Blaise Pascal. Pascal argued that a rational person should live as though God existed and seek to believe in God. The argument is that if God does not exist, such a person will have only a finite loss. A loss of whatever pleasures he may find while alive. In contrast, if God does exist, he stands to receive infinite gains, represented by eternity in Heaven, and avoid an eternity in Hell. This argument is trivial to debunk, however. The idea does not account for all other world views and beliefs a person may have other than that of the notion of God. One could think of an infinite number of ideas about reality a person could have that would make it preferable to act as if they were true rather than not. But that belief in itself would not make such claims any more truthful. If you genuinely wish to find truth in this world, start by accepting the finality of death. Only by admitting that this is your only shot at life can you start appreciating it properly. Your time is finite. Use it wisely.

Bitcoin can and probably will make you question your choices, forcing you to re-evaluate everything due to its absolutely finite nature. This is not limited to your spending patterns but all your decisions. As a result, you'll develop a more stoic way of tackling life. Stoicism is an ancient philosophy that recognizes that a rewarding life is best spent practicing the cardinal virtues — prudence, justice, fortitude, and temperance — while pursuing harmony with nature. Not only the nature around you but the nature of yourself. It teaches you to focus more on what you can change and less on what you can't. In Stoicism, virtue is the only good for human beings. External things, such as health, wealth, and pleasure, are neither good nor bad in themselves but have value as "material for virtue to act upon." This belief system aligns with how bitcoin will resonate in your psyche. Will bitcoin then turn us all into stoics? Probably not. But it will free up time for every single user and allow each of us to contemplate life's more profound questions. Which is something that many people yearn for in our age of mindless consumerism. People who have taken a step back and tried to view their lives through a philosophical lens are generally harder to fool than those who haven't. Thinking people are less likely to jump off cliffs like lemmings. Less likely to be content with living in a cage. The wolf will always be the bad guy through the eyes of a sheep. But sheep are rarely aware of their shepherd's intention to slaughter them all. Don't be a sheep or a lemming. Be sovereign.

6

MEMETICS

EVOLUTIONARY biologist Richard Dawkins coined the word *meme* in his book "The Selfish Gene" from 1976. The term is a variant of the word "gene." It refers to how ideas behave like DNA in many ways. Ideas, much like genes, either survive and reproduce or die out and become forgotten. Genes and memes well adapted to their environments have a better shot at reproducing and surviving than those ill-adapted. Memes are viral phenomena that evolve by natural selection analogous to biological evolution. They spread through behaviors that they generate in their hosts. An idea, for instance, can survive and thrive because people tell each other about it. Some ideas become extinct, while others survive, spread, and mutate. The perpetuation of ideas depends on how well they proliferate. Note that whether the idea is good or bad for the host's survival doesn't matter much, so long as the concept itself survives. Like parasitic life forms, human thoughts have an evolutionary process of their own. It is a process that can be more or less detached from the host's evolution. Put another way, bad ideas can survive for a long time too. Consider organized religions, organized crime, and the organized confiscation scheme of taxation. These concepts have flourished over a long span of history, but their hosts may not have. Ideas don't have to be truthful or beneficial to believers to survive. Successful memes remain and spread like genes, whereas unfit ones stall and fade away. Thus, memes that prove more effective at replicating and surviving stay in the meme pool. Don't confuse this meme pool with bitcoin's *mempool*,[1] by the way. Even though the two have some similarities.

The longer a meme or an idea stays in its host, the higher its chances of survival. A meme's lifetime gets extended every time its host broadcasts it to other minds. A meme that increases the longevity of its hosts will generally survive longer. Conversely, a meme that shortens the longevity of its hosts will tend to disappear faster. Despite this, transmissibility is more critical to the meme itself than the survival of its host. This is, after all, the only thing a meme needs to survive. The concept of suicide bombing is an example of a meme detrimental to its hosts. The idea survives because of the attention its host's death gets. Not its host's survival. Thus the act itself provides its own transmissibility.

A similar example from the biological world would be the sting of the common honey bee. The individual bee dies after using its stinger. The swarm survives, and therefore, so do the genetics required to spawn suicidal stingers. The genes that put the stinger on the bee in the first place. Both genes and memes are more powerful evolutionary entities than their respective hosts. Life-forms copy genetic

---

[1]Bitcoin's mempool is a virtual waiting room in which valid pending transactions are collected until a miner processes them to be added in the next block. Each node maintains its own mempool, in which data about unconfirmed transactions are kept until they get included in a block. The transactions in the mempool most well adapted to their environment have a greater chance at surviving too. In bitcoin, being well adapted usually means having a high fee attached. Anyway, let's get back to discussing memes.

information from parent to child. But genetic information can also spread through viruses and similar means. Memetic information, or ideas, can replicate in even more ways. Memes reproduce by copying themselves from one mind to another. Exposing your brain to a meme or a concept makes you a vessel for the evolution of that particular idea. Now, what separates the idea of bitcoin from other memes? A lot. First of all, bitcoin is nothing but a meme. Nothing but an idea. It is the idea that there exists a fixed set of rules that we can build our societies around. It is a layer of absolute truthfulness, robust enough to carry the whole world economy on its shoulders.

Moreover, it acts as a spawning pool for other memes. Other memes that help their parent meme, bitcoin, thrive and grow. How bitcoin owners perceive bitcoin doesn't matter to the idea itself. If the idea takes root in the human brain, it does. As soon as it does, that brain becomes a part of the network, a part of the meme. Bitcoin, the idea, is much larger than bitcoin, the computer network. And bitcoin, the computer network, wouldn't exist without the former. The beauty of the idea of bitcoin is that it grows even when people try to argue against it. Every time someone utters the word "bitcoin," the idea spreads. People remember hearing it and become more curious about it as it rises in value over time. They note that it's not going away and always comes back stronger after a crash. Those who already own bitcoin have an even greater incentive to spread the word about it. Doing so rewards them directly. They can "pump their bags," as the saying goes. Also, bitcoiners point out the flaws of the dominant monetary meme, fiat currency. Since bitcoin is truth represented by numbers, this is hard to argue against.

Most people don't realize that bitcoin is more than the sum of its parts. Bitcoin the word, bitcoin the idea, bitcoin the meme, and bitcoin the network are all parts of the same phenomenon. In this sense, bitcoin the t-shirt is the same phenomenon as bitcoin the protocol. So is bitcoin, the coffee mug. And the Lightning Network. Even gold bug dinosaur bitcoin critics are a part of bitcoin. It's all connected. It is an idea so powerful that nothing can stop it. A statement that helps its hosts survive by increasing their chances of survival. It ensures its own survival and that of its hosts by enriching them.

An individual bitcoin user is inescapably woven into his bitcoin when you think about it. Not only in the sense that the bitcoins are non-confiscatable but also in the sense that they are the same entity. When knowing is owning, the line between a bitcoin and the human being that holds it fades away. If you lose all information about a private key, you lose the bitcoins the key unlocks. In other words, if the only location the key to your bitcoins exists in is your mind, you are your bitcoins. If you haven't figured out a way to pass them on when you die, they're removed from the market. This means that their value passes on to everyone else in the network instead of your descendants. You and your bitcoins are in a symbiotic relationship. This bond grows stronger over time. Right now, it's a one-way relationship. Your bitcoins can't survive without you. In a hyperbitcoinized world, chances are that you won't be able to survive without your bitcoins. You can't overstate the power of this idea and the inevitability of its success. Because of how memes spread, nothing in this world is more powerful than an idea whose time has come, as Victor Hugo once eloquently put it.

After the year 2140, the total number of bitcoins on the market will only go down. By this point, almost everyone on the planet will own at least a couple of satoshis. When you think about it, it's not even possible to acquire that many, because of the fixed supply. If all bitcoins were split equally among the world's population, each person would have around 262 500 satoshis. That's twenty-one million times a hundred million, divided by eight billion. Of course, every person's net worth will never be equal. Nor should it be. Money should be a fair representation of your talents and effort. 262 500 is a tiny number. And the actual number is even smaller than that. Blockchain data suggests that the network has lost about five million bitcoins already. Another huge chunk has been off the market for more than five years. It is easy to underestimate the upcoming *Sat squeeze*. As the number of bitcoin users grows, so does the number of wallets and addresses. The more users and addresses, the more likely they will get lost in one way or another. The same leverage in the system that would typically take down a bank and have the government come in and reset the whole thing at the expense of its citizens now instead has the opposite characteristic. It reinforces the bearer asset (bitcoin) and increases its price. A single bitcoin can be lost, but its value remains. So make sure you hold your own keys. Your life may literally depend on it at some point.

People lose their bitcoins all the time. For example, they forget their passwords and lose their seed phrases. They also die and take their bitcoins with them. Pair this with the fact that bitcoins become more distributed over time. Bitcoin is a wealth distribution machine. Indeed, the number of bitcoin addresses with ten thousand bitcoins is shrinking, while the number of bitcoin addresses with one bitcoin or fewer is snowballing. In other words, bitcoin channels wealth from the rich to the poor by doing the opposite of what those claiming to be "redistributing wealth" do. Wealth would not need to be redistributed if it was distributed correctly in the first place. Reverse socialism is doing what the socialists themselves could never accomplish. Anyway, the point is that over time, bitcoins will get lost. There's no getting around that.

The phrase "don't forget to like and subscribe" has become a meme because of one thing. The profit motive behind it. Even if most YouTubers never break even, they still use the phrase. YouTubers strive for more followers and more attention. This is how powerful a meme with an attached profit incentive can be. Bitcoin, the meme, is unstoppable. Imagine how powerful the word "bitcoin" is because of the profit motive. Every bitcoin hodler has something to gain from the success of everything bitcoin-related. What is even more mind-blowing is the realization that bitcoin is self-sufficient in this way. Bitcoin, the meme, the network, the protocol, the philosophy, and bitcoin the party trick. Bitcoin, the idea, insult, joke, coffee mug, religion, and war cry. They're all the same phenomenon. Bitcoin and its surrounding ecosystems are all aspects of the same thing. The success of bitcoin as one fuels its success as all the others. It is a truly remarkable thing. There is no longer a clear-cut barrier between the informational and the physical realm. There is no boundary between memes and objects anymore. There's no way to separate subjective experience from objective reality. Bitcoin has illuminated how our thoughts about the world, and the world itself, are inseparable. It is humanity's most profound idea ever. Once you "get it," it becomes crucial for you to stop what you're doing at that moment and start helping this reality come into being. The more of us that do, the more life-altering the meme becomes. Once you've experienced bitcoin's superiority over everything else, there is no going back. It will change you much more than you can change it. Much, much more since you can't change it at all. Moreover, it will change everyone else as well. Absolutely everyone. It is only a matter of time.

Ideas are everything. They are at the core of everything we do and how we perceive the world around us. Everything humanity has ever accomplished was preceded by one or more thoughts in a single individual's head. The most potent ideas connect with reality on many levels. They give us a more accurate picture of the world and influence how it works. An inter-subjective belief system can make large groups work towards a common goal. The idea of "God" is an example of this. So is the idea of enlightenment. Whether these common goals are of benefit to the individual is another matter. But every inter-subjective belief system emerged as an idea. Whether they accurately represent reality or not doesn't matter in this sense. The point is that nothing can change the course of humanity as much as a great idea. When an idea arrives powerful enough to change the world, you can respond in one of two ways. The first way is to deny its existence. Despite what they might think, this is how most people respond. The other is embracing the idea and letting your innate curiosity explore it. But to do that, you must first determine whether an idea is essential enough to pay attention to. This is the tricky part. Separating signal from noise.

Actions speak louder than words. When money is manipulated, separating signal from noise becomes significantly more difficult. As resources get more misallocated over time, the entire societal landscape becomes harder to navigate. Price signals are supposed to reflect the will of the market. Which, by definition, is the will of the people, as far as what they can afford to want. A price is the best indicator of whether something is worth doing or not. Prices are not memes but representations of individual human beings' recent value hierarchies. It is important to remember that prices are historical data, not absolute truths in the present. Prices are never set in stone. A new price can always be negotiated.

People are so used to fixed prices for everyday items that they've almost forgotten this basic fact in modern society. When money is manipulated, price dynamics change. We're constantly being told to pay the men behind the curtain as little attention as possible. This inevitably leads to more power to them and less to the gullible masses. And a more impenetrable curtain. Bad things happen when people put more faith in their overlords and less in their own abilities. More coercion and less cooperation is the inevitable outcome. An unsustainable system cannot unfold in any other way. As time goes by, nation-states will have to become more totalitarian. More controlling. There's no other way to sustain an unsustainable system.

I still remember traveling to Mozambique as a child. We flew a brand new Boeing 747. Mid-flight, my younger brother and I were invited to the cockpit, to which there was no door separating the pilots from the passengers. There was a dark blue drape, but that was it. Inside the cockpit, we saw all sorts of buttons and knobs, which two kids could have easily fiddled with out of curiosity. But people weren't afraid. No one had ever heard of a terrorist hijacking a plane or a virus preventing people from flying. People managed their own risks. If you were afraid of flying, terrorists, viruses, or anything else, you could simply choose to not fly. Today, airports are incredibly meticulous in examining every passenger and their belongings. Everyone is considered a threat until they've proven that they're not. All these perceived threats are memes too. Any idea that can invoke fear in the human brain has a high chance of propagating and taking root in our collective consciousness. It is easy to plant the idea of a threat in a human brain but very hard to remove it again.

Furthermore, perceived threats make people easier to control. These phenomena might not come to be because of some grand conspiracy, but they sure are convenient tools for politicians with sociopathic tendencies. The more fearful the population, the more draconian laws can be enforced upon them. It's a downward spiral. The more totalitarian laws, the more frightened the public. The more frightened the people, the easier it is to encroach on their freedoms. All of this is, at least partly, a result of unsound money. A lack of truthfulness in the very base layer of all societies. But now there's another meme around. One that has the opposite effect.

Fiat currency is a meme. Like everything else in human society, it started as an idea. But the inner workings of fiat currency are not generally understood by people. The concept of bitcoin revolves around people's understanding of it. The twenty-one million coin supply cap is central to the whole idea. If you know just one thing about bitcoin, it's probably that. The only thing hindering bitcoin from becoming the world's dominant reserve currency is people's lack of understanding of its superiority. Fortunately, it is only a matter of time before this superiority becomes apparent to everyone. How could it not? The circle turned out to be the perfect shape for the wheel, and bitcoin is the ideal arrangement for sound money. Once you see it, there's no going back. There is no such thing as too much or too fast bitcoin adoption. The sooner hyperbitcoinization happens, the better.

Contrary to popular belief in many bitcoin circles, a more rapid adoption might be less violent than a slower one. After all, one of the most fantastic perks of bitcoin adoption is that it removes the incentive for violence on every level of society. The faster this happens, the smoother the transition. Not the other way around. This is why I personally think that education is so important. We'll all be better off if we can educate as many people as possible as soon as possible. Especially politicians. There will inevitably be bumps on the road to more bitcoin adoption. As hyperbitcoinization unfolds, some jurisdictions will try to ban the use of bitcoin. It is important to remember how absurd this is. Bitcoin is nothing but mathematics and communication.

Making bitcoin use illegal is as ridiculous as making calculus illegal. All you need to receive any amount of bitcoin is a random 256-bit number. That's what a bitcoin private key is. If you play rock, paper scissors 256 times and record the results, you've made a bitcoin wallet. If you toss a coin 256 times, you've created a bitcoin wallet. Heads or tails, ones or zeroes. How could a law prevent people from generating random numbers? Such a law would be highly absurd. A public key can easily be derived from a private one using elementary mathematics. And a bitcoin transaction is nothing but a message saying, "I move X amount of satoshis from this address to this one, here's my private key allowing me to do this, and I've signed this off here, using my private key." This is all bitcoin is. Banning "anonymous wallets" makes no sense. Banning a particular message type makes no sense, and banning mathematics certainly makes no sense either.

By erasing the distinction between knowing and owning, bitcoin is illuminating an often forgotten fact about trading. Trading *is* communicating. All exchanges are communication, and all communication is trade. Bitcoin is pointing out what should have been obvious all along. Property rights are everything. There can be no freedom of expression in a society that doesn't allow free trade. Everything but property rights is a political facade designed to justify unjust conduct. There's a civilized way to interact with other people and an uncivilized way. One is voluntary, the other is not. Bitcoin's apolitical nature points the finger at the real problem. Freedom of expression must include every non-violent way of communicating. A law banning bitcoin hints at what kind of a country you live in. Are you free? Is anyone?

7

SYMBIOSIS

In the Venom movies, actor Tom Hardy plays a reporter named Eddie Brock. He stumbles into a suspicious-looking lab in the first movie and gets "infected" by an alien life form. Mr. Brock and the alien then have to share the same body for the rest of the film. A somewhat schizophrenic relationship between their separate wills then unfolds. Eddie wants to keep living as a human being. The symbiote wants to eat brains. They also need each other. The alien needs Eddie's body to survive on Earth, and Eddie would be a pathetic loser if the alien left.

To add intrigue, the symbiote gives Eddie an array of superpowers, like very rapid regeneration of injured body parts, super strength, and vertical wall climbing. Once infected by the bitcoin virus, you'll experience a similar transformation as Eddie Brock. Once you've understood its underlying concepts, bitcoin will change your life. Soon enough, it'll become hard to imagine life without bitcoin and hard to deny the superpowers it gives you. Bitcoin provides you with self-sovereignty through its absolute scarcity and non-confiscatable nature. An amazing superpower. No known entity on Earth can change the fundamental principles of bitcoin. The rate of coin issuance and the coin cap of not quite twenty-one million bitcoins cannot, and will not, change. This is the source of each individual bitcoin owner's superpowers. It makes us impervious to the whims of power-hungry politicians and central bankers. We are not affected by them. "We... are bitcoin." The mere thought of sound money through absolute mathematical scarcity affects our minds too. Our relationship with time changes. We become less inclined to buy frivolous things and more inclined to save our money for the future. This transformation is not only wishful thinking on behalf of a bit-coin maximalist. Studies show this to be true. We can't help seeing the world through these new, faceted eyes of our new, alien companion. They show us how the current system has fooled every citizen in it. How "price stability" is an illusion. They show us the extent of our collective enthrallment and reveal the spell we've been under. The ugly face of fractional reserve banking, unveiled. But we... are bitcoin. We do not bow to any self-proclaimed ruler. Together, we control our destiny.

The notion of bitcoin being a part of its users is more than mere fiction. If you are the only one who knows how to unlock them, it is more than a metaphor. A bitcoin whose private key is in a person's head only is that person. Bitcoin, the element, is in a symbiotic relationship with its host. It is not only an element but a life-form. This is not the first time bitcoin has been compared to a living thing, far from it. People have called it a honey badger, an ant-hill, a swarm of cyber-hornets, mycelia, and a virus. But in this memory sense, it's a symbiote. It is a part of its host, and its host is part of it.

Bitcoins are in terminal symbiotic relationships with their hosts. Unless they are transferred to another host, bitcoins are taken off the market when their hosts die. Rediscovering a lost private key is like finding a needle in the Andromeda galaxy. The probability that anyone will ever find a lost one is so low that it's neglectable. However, the value of the network stays the same. In other words, the value of the lost bitcoins increases the value of all remaining bitcoins on the market by the same amount as those lost. People ought to be more careful with their coins. Backups and multi-sig solutions can protect you from disastrous mishaps. But the thought of bitcoin as a symbiote has many more profound philosophical consequences. As discussed earlier, bitcoin, the meme, the idea, the network, the token, and its users are the same thing. They're all different aspects of the same phenomenon. This means that as bitcoins' users change their behavior, so does bitcoin.

The more invested you are in bitcoin, the more you change. And there are many different ways to do this. Writers like me connect to bitcoin the idea, and bitcoin the meme, in more ways than via our tokens. The success of our writings depends on the success of bitcoin too. Our essays help bitcoin, the meme, propagate. At least, that's what we hope will happen. Investors in bitcoin-related companies have yet other connections to it. Today, pension funds hold bitcoin. Everyone who has part of their savings invested in such a fund is linked to the success of bitcoin. In fact, they too are bitcoin, even though they're probably not aware of it. On a long enough time scale, bitcoin will change them all. Bitcoin will lower their time preference.

Living in a symbiotic relationship with bitcoin also changes your perception of yourself. Your actual self that is. Your ego. What shitcoiners call "toxic bitcoin maximalism" is the symbiotes' immune system. It makes the symbiote and its hosts resistant to bullshit. The absolute truth protocol provides you with a defense mechanism against bullshit. When you learn about how fiat currencies come to be, you begin questioning everything else. A "follow the money" attitude ensues. You stop swallowing the processed sludge of the mainstream media outlets, and you start doing more research on your own. "Bitcoin maximalists" are the way they are because they did their homework. You become one by following the white rabbit all the way down the hole. By questioning everything about the system. By examining every possible attack vector against bitcoin. Only then will you be reborn with the necessary conviction to exit fiat for good. As a bitcoiner, you have to be your own most savage critic because you're the one in charge. This usually makes the bitcoiner more of a skeptic in other areas too. Through bitcoin, the lens, the nudity of all emperors become blatantly apparent.

Bitcoin users develop a lower time preference over time. It is one of the most life-changing transformations you can experience. The symbiote gives its host an incentive to save rather than spend. It is, in itself, a savings technology. It is all about time preference. The higher your time preference, the more you let instinct dictate your behavior. A person with the highest time preference imaginable is a feral beast. When you have no savings, you can't plan for the future. Your first priority becomes feeding yourself. People with a high time preference have no choice but to act in very egocentric ways. Fear dictates their actions. The more you can save, the more predictable the future becomes. The more you can plan ahead, the less barbaric you can afford to be.

Time preference is directly connected to civility. This is not rocket science. Nor is it brain surgery. It is a science called praxeology, and it's not taught in any public schools. It is the study of human action. The science of why human beings take deliberate action. It's about what triggers us to seek means and reach ends. There's a reason that this subject is not in any public school curricula. Praxeology eloquently describes how coercive funding methods detriment society at large. But that is a subject for another chapter. The point here is the direct connection between time preference and morality. Once again, a relationship between information, time, and ethics. The more information you have about the future, the lower your time preference. A lowering of it can allow you to afford a higher moral standard.

Many bitcoiners tell a similar falling-down-the-bitcoin-rabbit-hole story. As they tumble down, their personalities change for the better. It's pretty simple. Bitcoin's Number-go-Up technology makes you wealthier by doing nothing over long periods. This, in turn, removes your spending urges to a high degree. In other words, you become rich the old-fashioned way. By saving for the future. Delayed gratification. Also, many bitcoiners become curious about what goes on behind the curtains of the world. The bitcoin transmogrifier creates stoic superheroes. Alphas without fear, ready to face the world and all its perils. A person injected with hope. A more spiritual, philosophical, calm, and less cynical human being.

Not to mention how friendly bitcoiners become to each other. It is hard to even come up with any downsides to this transformation. My personal journey has been one of several jaw-drop moments at the sheer generosity of my fellow bitcoiners. This all relates to the fact that all aspects of bitcoin are merely different aspects of the same phenomenon. Bitcoin attracts high-quality people but also helps every person become better. Helping the cause is helping yourself, which is helping humanity at large. To us bitcoiners, the thought of a society without violent coercion is now not only a possibility. It is an inevitability. There's no going back when you realize the true power of an idea whose time has come. Hyperbitcoinization is happening. You're living through it. It is a fantastic time to be alive, especially for those of us who treasure freedom and property rights. Never forget that. Cynicism is a dead end. The world may seem bleak at times, but there are many reasons to be hopeful. Bitcoin can help you see them.

When your mind is the only place where information about your bitcoin exists, you are your bitcoins. This means that you take them with you to the grave when you die. Imagine that a person memorizes their seed phrase before *cryo-freezing* their head when they die. They could keep on hodling while dead and spend their bitcoin again when resurrected! Provided that cryo-resurrection ever becomes a reality, of course. Hal Finney, the first person to ever receive a bitcoin from someone, had his head cryo-frozen when he passed away. Of course, you don't even need something as outlandish as a defrosted head to imagine a dead person hodling.

What about someone buried in a casket with a steel seed plate? When a bitcoin is off-market, it's off-market. It doesn't matter if it's removed entirely or if someone's holding on to it for later use. The effect on the remaining coins on the market is the same. Less supply, same demand, higher price. True, frozen heads aren't likely to wake up and remember things anytime soon. But there's a point to thinking about such scenarios anyway. They illuminate that hodling is a very peculiar action. Saving is not the same as hodling. Saving is the deliberate act of delaying your gratification. Hodling can be, but it doesn't have to be. As mentioned above, dead people can hodl.

In fact, all inanimate objects that can store information can hodl. Hodling is an activity that is not exclusive to human beings. Chimpanzees can memorize twenty-four words. They wouldn't know what to do with them, but they could hodl bitcoin. Removing bitcoins from the market decreases the total amount of bitcoins in circulation. In other words, bitcoins become more scarce over time. More and more bitcoins disappear from the market every day. There is no way of knowing if they're lost forever or not. If someone intends to use them at a later date or not. But it doesn't matter. The result is the same. A scarcer asset. Less supply. If the demand for bitcoins goes up or stays the same, the price will increase. But there's even more to hodling than this. Hodling bitcoin is not the same as having a gold bar under your mattress. You can store bitcoins under your bed too, but it's not the only way to hold a bitcoin key. The imagination of the individual hodler is the only thing limiting the number of ways you can hodl. Bitcoins are informational. You can program them. Memorize them. Communicate them. You can even convert them into Morse code if you want. The possibilities are endless.

The informational realm is not restricted by the laws of physics in the same way as the physical realm. We remove all physical barriers by relocating the notion of ownership into the informational realm. Barriers that limit what we can and cannot do as market actors. A bitcoin doesn't care about distances. Nor does it care about gravity. It enables global trust. Imagine trust being embroidered into the very fabric of society. As I write these words, anyone with three bitcoins or more can buy or build a house in El Salvador and claim ownership of it. And get a permanent residency in the country along with the bargain. All by clicking a few buttons on a keyboard. Without any middlemen or rent-seekers.

El Salvador is the first domino to fall in a game never seen before in human history. A global nation state's prisoner's dilemma is now a reality. The only rational action a nation can take is to hop on to the bitcoin train as soon as possible. Before other countries do. This is now an actual situation that all nation-states and central banks will have to deal with. The sooner they adopt bitcoin, the better off they'll be. It will be the beginning of the end for them, of course, but it's still the best move they can make. For the first time in history, individuals have a chance to front-run entire nation-states. And multinational corporations. The most significant wealth migration ever known to man has begun. For the first time in history, that money flows in the opposite direction of what we're used to. For the first time in history, it is all voluntary. Finally, the individual human being is elevated to the center stage. Alongside her loyal companion symbiote, absolute trust.

In the fiat monetary system, you have two main options to get rich. The first is taking on debt and acquiring assets like stocks, bonds, and real estate. This is the unmistakable winning move when interest rates approach zero. And they're approaching zero everywhere. In some places, interest rates are even openly negative. In others, they're suspiciously low on paper but negative when you take inflation into account. The other way to get wealthy in the fiat monetary system is to play the game of politics. To move ahead in a political career, you must drop all your actual opinions and adopt whatever views your party wants you to advance. A narrative set by political correctness and funding from lobbyists. As a politician, you can enjoy a high salary set by other politicians and funded by taxes and inflation imposed on the public by other politicians. It's a game of connections, and those closest to the money spigot or ruling party wins.

Providing goods and services to your fellow man, which they actually asked for, is usually not an efficient way to get rich in the fiat system. Sometimes, people get rich by providing things that people ask for because of government subsidies, but those things hardly count. Electric cars and solar panels are examples of such goods. They would both be far less prevalent if they weren't subsidized. The more into the future we get, the more bitcoin will replace fiat. This will turn the tables entirely and force people to provide value to each other. Using violence and coercion will no longer be profitable the way it is now.

A person's political leaning is an indicator of to what extent they're willing to use violence. They might not see things this way themselves, but this is what politics is. It's not a scale from right to left. That scale is not relevant. It's about how much coercion society allows. Communists and socialists want completely obedient citizens who prioritize the collective's interests over their own. To achieve this, every person has to be coerced into doing whatever task they're assigned. They're willing to act violently upon peaceful people to acquire and gain control over every aspect of society, from energy to clothing to housing to food to everything else. Modern "liberals," politically known as the American left and most European center-right parties, draw the line at universal healthcare. Modern conservatives are skeptical towards state-funded health care but okay with the state paying for unemployment insurance, retirement funds, healthcare and housing for the poor and the old, and public education. Classical liberals are rare these days, but most think the state should be as small as possible. In their view, that "minimal" state should still provide funding for the fire brigade, the roads, the police, the court system, and the military.

They all miss a crucial fact that both Ludvig von Mises and Murray Rothbard have pointed out. A small state is as much a utopian idea as the idea of no state at all. If not even more unrealistic. Once an organization is given a monopoly on violence in a society, no force can stop that organization from growing ever larger. All democracies, and indeed all dictatorships, monarchies, and theocracies too, inevitably devolve into totalitarian states at some point. The only way to stop this is to be ready to stand up for the most basic of moral principles. To not be willing to use violence against peaceful people, ever. To always seek acquisition of desired products and services through voluntary relationships. Not an easy task in this day and age. But way easier when you have superpowers. When you are bitcoin. And you indeed are your bitcoins. Make no mistake about it.

8

VIOLENCE

AN enslaved person is a person who another person treats as their property. They are not allowed to quit working for their owners. Nor are they allowed to work for anyone else. In the past, indebted people, people who broke the law, or people on the losing side of war, sometimes became enslaved. In other words, people usually became enslaved because someone forced them to. Slavery is rarely a voluntary state of being. Nor is it an either-or. Viewed through a libertarian lens, almost everyone is at least partially enslaved. If you're 100% enslaved, all the fruits of your labor go to your owner. You keep nothing. By extension, your physical well-being becomes a priority of your owner. At least for the duration of your enslavement. Regardless of your political opinions and how effective you think taxes are, it can be valuable to view how much you're giving away each month from an individual perspective.

You give away a specific part of your time and efforts when you pay taxes. In theory, taxes are giving something back to society at large. But you do not get to decide how the state allocates your confiscated resources. Viewed through this lens, you would be [insert your current tax rate here] percent enslaved, right? Wrong. Your income tax is not the only tax you're paying. Chances are high that you have to pay some other personal tax on top of that. Property tax, wealth tax, capital gains tax, inheritance tax, etcetera. So then, is this cumulative tax proportional to how much of an enslaved person you are? Nope. Your employer is paying taxes too. Chances are that the people you work for, be it your employer or your client, are paying a plethora of taxes themselves. Corporate taxes, capital gains taxes, social security contributions, etc. They have to get this money from somewhere. So chances are high that you're indirectly paying for their taxes also, through increased prices and fees. At least a part of them. Okay, are we done soon? Nope. If you live in an interventionist society, you're paying extra taxes every time you buy a good or service. Value-added taxes (VAT), sales taxes, import tariffs, environmental taxes. All the taxes paid during the manufacture and transportation of the goods you're buying. They all add to your total enslavement rate. But it doesn't end there either. We have to include inflation. The most devious tax of all. The tax that funnels wealth from the begging hands of the have-nots into the iron fists of the have-it-alls.

Government statisticians present inflation as a number. They calculate this number by looking at the cost of a bag of groceries from one year to another. This is a deliberate misleading of the public. In reality, inflation is a vector, always pointing upwards to some degree. Price inflation is proportional to the amount of new monetary units each year. It comes with a lag, but sooner or later, that new cash will increase your costs of living. The lion's share of the newly created, reallocated value of this new total money supply goes into luxury goods. Fine art, real estate in high-cost areas, these types of things.

The poor always end up paying for inflation. The proportion of the poor's total wealth held in cash is very high compared to the wealthy, who own assets that appreciate over time in fiat terms. Today, the actual monetary inflation of most countries is somewhere between

5% and 10%. And even higher than that in some cases. This may sound like a small problem, but it's a massive one in reality. First, everyone needs to make more than a 5%-10% profit every year to keep up with the inflation rate. If you don't, you're losing money. Everyone not getting a 10% raise per year pays for someone else's excesses through their labor. With as little as a five percent inflation rate, it takes only fourteen years to halve a currency's value. That's about as many years as it takes for Guns n' Roses to release a new album. Now add all these taxes and shadow taxes together. Are we then finally done with this bit of thought experiment? I'm afraid not because we've forgotten about a crucial side effect of taxation. Everyone's altered time preference.

Whenever the state imposes a tax on a person, that person increases his time preference. Like robbery, taxation forces us to adopt a higher time preference. A higher time preference means more short-term decision-making. With a reduced amount of room for afterthought, people can't plan ahead for the future. This leads to the misallocation of resources everywhere. Since every citizen suffers from an altered time preference, misallocation happens everywhere, all the time. The deeper into a tax-based society we get, the harder it becomes to separate the actual market signals from the noise of interventionist misspending. Goods and services are produced not because there's a market demand for them but because they're subsidized in one way or another. This never works. The "Trabant" is an excellent example of how centrally planned economies misallocate resources and produce crappy goods. The Trabant was a car made in the DDR between 1957 and 1991. After the fall of the Berlin Wall, it became apparent how inferior the Trabant was compared to vehicles produced in more market-liberal societies. Its inefficient, labor-intensive production line had only survived thanks to government subsidies. There was no place for the Trabant in a reunified German economy.

When governments intervene in markets, they repeat the mistakes the countries of Eastern Europe made in the latter half of the 20th century. High taxes on competing goods is a form of indirect subsidy too. It is impossible to calculate the total damage taxation and inflation have done to society. But think of it this way: If you're in a so-called *laissez-faire* country, your total taxes might look something like this - 25% income tax, 25% social-security contributions, and other taxes your employer pays. Even before we start adding hidden costs, that's about 50%. Add a VAT adjusted for certain goods with extra taxes, like fuel for your car, which you need to commute to and from work. That's an additional 25% of whatever you had left. So, in total, 62,5%. Make that 65% to compensate for every other tax we didn't include. Now add a best-case scenario 5% inflation rate on top of this.

Congratulations, you live in a "free country," and you're 70% a slave. But aren't we forgetting something here? Yes, we are! The so-called "public sector." The "public sector" consists of everyone on the receiving end of taxation. They pay taxes too, but this is merely a charade on behalf of the government. In reality, everyone working in the public sector is a net loss to society. Their income minus the taxes they pay plus the cost of the charade itself adds up to their total cost. The bureaucracy is expanding to meet the needs of the expanding bureaucracy. The lion's share of the public sector provides its "customers" with services no one ever asked for. It's either that or providing "services" whose sole function is to cement some other part of the bureaucratic machine. The opportunity cost for not allowing public sector employees to contribute to society by participating in the real labor market is enormous. Removing around half the population from participating in the free market makes that market half as productive, right? This, too, is a gross under-estimation. It is linear thinking, and market efficiency is not a linear thing. The market is a communications network. The value of a communications network is proportional to the number of its users, squared. The damage done by government intervention in markets is immeasurable.

Despite all these handicaps imposed by statism, market forces are still highly potent. Market forces are the reason that starvation is almost eradicated from Earth today. They are the reason that a device with access to all the world's knowledge, books, movies, tv shows, and music can now fit in your pocket. A device James Bond couldn't have dreamt of thirty years ago. No one on Earth can construct a mobile phone from scratch on their own. It's all because of free trade that such a device can exist at all. Milton Friedman once used a simple pencil to illustrate how these forces work. A simple pencil couldn't have come into existence without international trade. The wood, the black lead, and the paint finish of the pencil all come from different continents. No central planner or social engineer had anything to do with the pencil's production. It came to be because of its market demand and the division of labor enabled by the different price signals in the process. All this happened despite pervasive government interventionism going on in markets globally. If we define slavery as the percentage of our labor that we give up, we're all enslaved to the government to some extent. You might argue that this is not wholly a bad thing since the physical well-being of the enslaved person is a priority of its owner. Thus, the state must allow its subjects to keep some of their earnings to keep them alive. Think again. Controlling the masses can be very cheap. The less they have, the easier they are to manage. Universal Basic Income is a good indicator of how the state values its subjects. Under such a system, most people would be one hundred percent dependent on the state for their survival. This is the end goal of such policies, regardless of how they're being advertised. People dependent on wealth redistribution are unlikely to vote against such policies. They're no longer seen as people by the state but zombified voting cattle. The state grows bigger everywhere through mechanisms like Universal Basic Income, like a tumor. Add to this the fact that collectivists form larger groups than individualists. In this light, it's not hard to see that elections themselves are a leftist phenomenon. Holding a state-sanctioned popularity contest every four years does not make theft less immoral. Violent coercion is wrong, regardless of what "the majority" thinks.

So what can you, as an individual, do about all this? From within the system, not a lot, unfortunately. The less individualistic you are, the less independent of a mind you have, the easier it is for you to form large groups because you don't care that much what that group actually thinks. You're happy with walking in line and doing what you're told. This is the core problem of democracy. It favors sheep, not wolves. Lemmings will win elections and happily throw themselves off cliffs. Because of this, the more time that passes, the more draconian our societies will become. The more enslaved their citizens. The only thing we can do as individuals is focusing on the tools we have at hand. Bitcoin is the ultimate form of money since it has no ties to any state or institution. Being the best form of money is also the ultimate time-saving tool. The perfect freedom tool. And what are tools, if not freedom-enablers? Tools and technologies save time. And bitcoin does that job better than all other tools. In this sense, bitcoin is the best tool ever invented. Period. Unlike Universal Basic Income schemes, bitcoin is actually both universal and fundamental. Universal Basic Income is not universal, not basic, and definitely not income.

Many bitcoiners stress the importance of privacy. The risk of retroactive taxation from using your bitcoins is often emphasized. We're encouraged to use all the available privacy tools. Coin-joins, payment mixers, TOR routing, KYC-free coins, etc. While these privacy concerns are currently salient to a considerable extent, their proponents leave out a fundamental property of bitcoin. Number-go-Up technology. As a long-term hodler of bitcoin, you contribute to the scarcity of available coins on the market. This scarcity limits the supply, pushing the price upwards as demand grows. When the price goes up, you become wealthier. This core aspect of bitcoin opens up a lot of doors. It gives you options. Everyone has a price, including those who want to leech off your earnings. As time goes by and the cost of bitcoin goes up, you are more likely to be able to buy yourself out of dire situations.

Furthermore, bitcoin lobbyists will become more potent over time. Countries will experience increasing pressure to ease their bit-coin legislation because bitcoiners will mass migrate to more friendly jurisdictions. This is already happening. Many prominent bitcoiners are moving to countries like El Salvador and Mexico. Over time, chain analytics firms will become less and less dependent on their clients. More able to support themselves using their own stacks instead. Not to mention that the protocol itself gets more privacy-focused over time. Improvements such as the Lightning Network and Taproot are excellent for bitcoin privacy.

Significantly, this migration to bitcoin is defunding the nation-states themselves. Bitcoin is a waiting game. So is bitcoin privacy. As always, patience gets rewarded, and recklessness gets punished. In short, how a monetary system ought to function. The saying goes, "In this world, nothing is certain, except death and taxes." There is now a third certainty. Bitcoin. It functions as a protector against at least one of the other two.

Furthermore, the first two, death and taxes, are responsible for the most horrific activity mankind has ever designed - war. Warfare is by far the worst form of slavery. A soldier is not only forced into both risking and giving up vast parts of his own life. He's also obligated to deprive others of theirs. The chain of crimes involved in making a citizen of one country take the life of a citizen of another is long. From the thievery of taxation to the brainwashing machinery of public schooling. From the mass confiscation of resources through inflation to the slavery of conscription. All of this to deprive millions of potential trading partners of their lives. While simultaneously wasting resources on destroying as much property as possible. War is disgusting in every way imaginable. Preventing war from ever happening again should be on top of every thinking persons' agenda. To understand how to do that, we first need to know how armed conflicts occur in the first place. How do the sociopaths that rule us manage to fool us to the extent that we start killing each other? As discussed earlier, the illusion of an afterlife helps. So does the illusion of any "greater good," for that matter. But the most devious mechanism that made both world wars possible was inflation. Inflation has paid for the destruction of millions of lives throughout history.

The British, French, and German governments all took their countries off the gold standard in 1914. They did this to fund the mass murder effort that was World War I, which took over forty million human lives. It left vast parts of Europe in ruins, and post-war Germany, in particular, didn't fare well. After a series of mutinies by German sailors and soldiers, emperor Kaiser Wilhelm II lost the support of his military. The German people forced him to abdicate in 1918. This, and the treaty of Versailles in the summer of 1919, led to the formation of the Weimar Republic. The Weimar Republic's constitution included many rights that sounded good on paper. All citizens had the same civil rights and responsibilities. The right to freedom of expression. The right to peaceful assembly. The right to freedom of religion. No state church. State-run, public education, free and mandatory for children. The ownership of private property. The right to equal opportunity and earnings in the workplace. A constitution that could last for centuries, correct? Wrong.

Following the Treaty of Versailles, Germany's coal and iron ore production decreased. The costs of separating the nation after the war spiraled out of control, the German government could not pay its debts. Things got even worse when the industrious Ruhr area was occupied by French and Belgian forces. The Germans tried to resist the occupation by going on a government-mandated strike. More and more factories and plants were shut down, and the German economy tanked hard. The Weimar government responded in the only way it knew. They started printing more money. This led the republic to an even more catastrophic state of affairs - hyperinflation. The lion's share of the population lost all their savings, and mass poverty ensued. A black market barter economy was the only thing that kept people alive during this tragic era.

The republic managed to survive with the help of two people, liberal foreign minister Gustav Stresemann and a republican banker from Nebraska, Charles Dawes. Stresemann managed to repair the Weimar republic's diplomatic relations with France. He even managed to reduce its war debt to the allied nations. With the help of Dawes, he replaced the Mark with a new currency. The American-backed Rentenmark. "Dawes' Plan" loaned large sums of American bank money to the German economy. The loans permitted Germany to recover its industrial production. Reparation payments to France and Belgium as required by the Versailles Treaty ensued. But then, the Great Depression began on the other side of the Atlantic.

The Federal Reserve's "easy credit policy" had led to an unsustainable credit-driven boom. During this era, the inflation of the money supply spurred an untenable boom in asset prices and capital goods. When the Federal Reserve finally tightened its monetary policy in 1928, it was too late. Not only for the American economy but also for the Weimar Republic's economy, which was closely connected to the American one. Another economic depression soon followed. The German president at the time, Paul von Hindenburg, invoked Article 48 as a response. This article gave the president the power to override the Reichstag during "emergencies." Does this sound familiar to you? It should. When governments screw things up, it is not uncommon that they respond by giving themselves more power. After amassing about a third of the German votes in 1932, Adolf Hitler used Article 48 to provide himself and the National Socialist Party total control over the nation in 1933.

We all know what that led to. World War II was a tragedy that took around 75 million human lives and almost destroyed Europe. Germany had moved to yet another type of currency called the Reichsmark shortly before the war. The German government advertised the Reichsmark as a currency on a gold standard, but it really wasn't. In reality, this was far from true. Dummy companies were set up by the Nazis for the Reichsbank to issue more notes than for which it had gold in its reserves. Besides this, the currency was partly backed by property theft in invaded territories. Especially gold reserves. Much of the Third Reich's many victims' personal property was confiscated too. Gold, coinage, and other personal gold stuff were stolen from the jews especially. Gold teeth were torn from dead bodies. They melted it all down as bullion for the minting of new Reichsmark coins.

None of the warring countries could have afforded the wars without inflationary currencies. Not World War I and not World War II. Nor any other modern war effort for that matter. Not for more than a few months. During the twentieth century alone, the German people experienced nine different currencies. Think about that! One hundred years, nine types of media of exchange. The only pre-war currency was also the only one redeemable for gold, the Goldmark. All the succeeding ones have been inflationary. Stealing time and effort from currency users to pay for wars and indebting the country. Inflation always funnels wealth and power from the hands of the people into the hands of the elite. The elite can then use this power to sacrifice their citizens as pawns on a chessboard in war times.

This version of twentieth-century history might differ a bit from what they taught you in school. After all, history is written by the winners of the war. As a kid in Sweden during the eighties, we were taught that Sweden had nothing to do with the world wars. They told us that Sweden was a "neutral" country. During the cold war too. I've later come to learn that "race biology" was a term first coined in Uppsala, a university town close to Stockholm. But the most critical aspect of both world wars is never discussed in any public school, and for an understandable reason. Public schooling wouldn't survive for very long if people understood money. The giant missing piece from our history classes is the piece about money. How our governments managed to fund the wars. How people weren't fighting for a "greater good" at all, but for a bunch of psychopaths in suits. Without an institution telling you about the legitimacy of a government, you wouldn't buy their narrative. The flame of curiosity shines bright in almost all children. But is extinguished by the drudgery of public schooling. Would we have noticed the men behind the curtain if it weren't so? Some of us would. But it takes a very nerdy mind to realize what's going on in today's world.

To question who's pulling the strings, you must be interested in mathematics, history, and economics. A high level of curiosity is needed to even ask the question. Most people can't detect what's wrong with the system from within the system. Public schooling is part of the problem. The natural sciences in general, and engineering in particular, has made it possible for humans to put robots on the surface of Mars. Still, most humans on this planet haven't yet realized that theft is always wrong. Through this lens, it's mind-blowing how uncivilized we still are. The threat of war is omnipresent, always looming above us like a dark cloud on an otherwise blue sky. It will always be there as long as there's a link between government and money. The only way to end the perpetual threat of war is to separate money and state, once and for all.

The UK abandoned gold during the Napoleonic wars. The US went off the gold standard in 1971 to finance the war in Vietnam, among other things. In the nineties, the US declared war on Iraq. A country that wanted to abandon the petro-dollar system. The list goes on. An entity that can issue any amount of money at no cost to itself can be wasteful beyond our imagination. Not only can it fund the top consumers of fossil fuel on the planet, the military institutions. It can also misallocate resources to a disastrous extent. A so-called "public sector" can be as wasteful as it pleases without any consequences. Armies and navies consume vast amounts of resources in peacetime too. These institutions are designed to destroy lives and property. That's their only purpose. As long as there are nation-states, we'll always have these "big spender" arms races. Military and financial. Bad money and bad government go hand in hand. You can't have one without the other. The damage they've caused to the planet is immeasurable. Bitcoin functions as a force against them in many different ways. The more we use Bitcoin, the less we use government-issued fiat currencies. This means that the more we empower ourselves, the more we disempower the mafiosos of the elite.

A free market network utilizes all the brainpower connected to it. It is distributing cognition in this sense. What it produces is a signal. A price signal. This signal provides crucial information to all market actors. Information about how to best divide up their time and resources. The price signal tells participants in a market what to do. This makes the free market a vastly more intelligent decision-maker than any bureaucrat could ever dream of being. A central planner has one brain, and a committee may have ten. They can cause immeasurable damage by tampering with the price signal. The free market utilizes every brain, but the price signal gets blurred whenever a central planner interferes. This causes confusion and misallocates resources and human time.

Every time the property of one human is stolen, the market function degrades. The act of confiscation raises the victims' time preference. At the same time, it removes accountability from the thief. In other words, the act of appropriation disrupts the entire price signaling mechanism. Both for the thief and their victim. This then distorts the price signal given to the rest of the market's participants. In short, theft always leads to the misallocation of time and resources. The use of violence, or a threat thereof, in one part of a market leads to dishonesty in another. When inflation hits a good producer so that his profits can no longer pay for his living costs, he must choose between three dishonest options. He can increase the product's price, reduce the amount of product per unit sold, or reduce the quality of his goods. None of these choices is an ethical one. Now take into account that inflation affects every single market participant. Every single human being. Violent intervention in the forms of taxation and inflation is everywhere. Its net outcome is always negative. Bitcoin gives you the option to bypass them. Its non-confiscatable nature removes incentives for violence on every level of society. Whether you're a pick-pocket or the US army doesn't matter. Being violent against others is not as profitable as it used to be. This will improve everyone's quality of life as it will improve the functionality of each and every market.

Violent interventionism in the form of coercive taxes and inflation is everywhere. These phenomena handicap the global free market. Interest rates kept low by artificial means give rise to global monopolies. Giant conglomerates in cahoots with big governments. The current state of the world is one where one percent of the population owns half of all the assets. This is the inevitable outcome of unlimited money printing. It is ridiculous how much better humanity could do if we solved this problem. Bitcoin is the solution we need and deserve. We're witnessing the transition playing out in real-time.

Life on this Earth evolved through competition. At first, evolution was an outright battle between one-celled organisms. Whatever organism managed to survive long enough to reproduce survived. But a peculiar thing happened the first time two cells stuck together. By working together rather than fighting each other, these two cells had a greater chance of surviving than single ones. Cooperation had been born. Soon, organisms grew, and evolutionary biology began. Those life-forms that were most efficient at projecting energy and reproducing survived. Those that couldn't keep up died out. Fast forward a couple of million years, and you find humans. Fighting each other and cooperating with each other to varying degrees. Humans have evolved beyond mere fangs, beaks, and claws. We have developed gigantic prefrontal cortices, which we can use to design and construct much more dangerous weapons. Weapons that can't even be used without wiping out our entire species, such as nuclear bombs.

This has left the human race in a peculiar situation. A stalemate. No holder of atomic bombs can ever aggress against another nuclear power without committing suicide in the process. Therefore, we launch proxy wars instead. A proxy war is an armed conflict between two states or non-state actors who act on the instigation or on behalf of other parties not directly involved in the hostilities. Poor people in poor countries are paying a high price for the power games of the super-rich. Nuclear weapons prevent potential aggressors from attacking the soil of the countries that own them. They do this by merely revealing that they exist at all. They're not cheap to produce. A potential attacker understands that a failed attack would be a very costly affair. In this sense, weapon arsenals and standing armies serve the same purpose for humans as antlers or tusks for animals. Evolutionary Proof-of-Work, if you will.

"War, what is it good for? Absolutely nothing!" Or is it? Well, history is written by the winners of wars, and they get to set the rules for everyone else. When Richard Nixon decoupled the dollar from gold in 1971, other nations could do little about it. The American military was the dominant force in the world then as it is now. Therefore, the United States decides the rules of the global trade game. But what about the future? For how long can this empire last? All great civilizations end at some point, and so will our current Western Societies. We're already beginning to see the cracks in the facade. This time around, though, there's another way of showing off your dominance than brute force. Today, we have digital antlers. Digital armies. Even digital nukes. Bitcoin's Proof-of-Work system can function as all three. As hyperbitcoinization progresses, the world's superpowers will have no choice but to join the global battle for hashing power. In doing so, they employ a new kind of army or develop a new type of atomic bomb, if you will. For what is Proof-of-Work, if not a display of how ironclad the fortress around your assets is? It's a literal digital arms race without the need to spill the blood of a single human soul. The stalemate is now broken since there's another way to sacrifice energy to compete for dominance than investing in a large military force. All a nation needs to do is connect a couple of *ASICs* to the electricity grid. After they do, attacks against them become less profitable. Moreover, they'll be less prone to attack others since more resources would be allocated to the miners and fewer to the military industry.

The most remarkable aspect of money's migration from the physical realm into the informational one is that it removes the profit motive from violent behavior on all levels of society. It obsoletes the burglar as well as the taxman. The mafiosos as well as the armies of the world. First, they ignore you, then they laugh at you, then they fight you, then you win. We are now in the "then they fight you" phase, and it's kind of obvious who the long-term winner will be. One day, the 20th and early 21st centuries will be looked back on by our children and grandchildren, who will be appalled by our uncivilized brutal ways. In hindsight, humans always condemn excessive violence. No one is proud of the Vietnam war, slavery, Nazi Germany, Communist Russia, or the genocide of the indigenous peoples of America. Post hyperbitcoinization, our descendants will be embarrassed by how their ancestors behaved violently against one another. Coercive taxes and inflation will be viewed as brutal, barbaric practices of a dark past. Make sure you're on the right side of history. The path to freedom seldom leads through more obedience.

9

DEFLATION

A *shitcoin* is a form of currency that is more or less designed to enrich its creators. It differs from bitcoin in this sense because bitcoin's creator has disappeared, and their known coins have never moved. Shitcoins can be subdivided into two main categories: *Craptocurrencies* and *Kleptocurrencies*. Craptocurrencies are exercises in cryptographic mental gymnastics. Deliberate scams trying to piggyback off of the success of bitcoin. Craptocurrencies are also known as *altcoins* or "cryptos." Names that give them more credit than they deserve. These are all pyramid schemes and scams. Their creators fool ignorant newcomers into giving them their bitcoins. They do this mainly by claiming that "blockchain technology" has more than one use case.

Some of the earliest descriptions of bitcoin revolved around arbitrary properties, like "Payments per second" and "merchant adoption." Neither is that important for an entirely new type of money. Cryptocurrency creators use these misconceptions to push their own narrative. There's no real point in using a blockchain for anything but bitcoin. A blockchain is nothing but a slow database designed to do one thing: Ensure that bitcoins cannot be double-spent. To grasp the implications of what this means, view bitcoin as a discovery. Absolute mathematical scarcity achieved by consensus in a sufficiently decentralized distributed network was a discovery rather than an invention. It cannot be achieved again by a network made up of participants aware of this discovery, since the very thing discovered was resistance to replicability itself. The idea that there will always be many types of money with different use cases is wrong. It's based on a misunderstanding of what money is in the first place. Money is the most saleable good in society. It is a winner takes all game. You can trade money for every other good and service there is. There's not even a need for a plural form of the word. With bitcoin, we now know the upper limit of how much value a single unit of money could theoretically represent. Everything, divided by twenty-one million.

As in all emerging markets, many opportunists start businesses when they see a new asset arise. Some exchanges and wallet providers realized something a few years after bitcoin was discovered. Selling bitcoins for other currencies wasn't a very profitable business model. Especially not since accumulating more bitcoins turned out to be the apparent right path forward. The quickest way of getting your hands on more bitcoins was to sell cheap clones and copies of it to the ignorant masses. Because of this, many early exchanges and wallet providers morphed into shitcoin casinos. If you've been in this space for a couple of years already, you probably know which ones. Some of the most significant wallet providers in 2016 have now turned into complete clownware.

Craptocurrencies come in many shapes and forms. Some of them claim to increase privacy. Some claim they make transactions cheap and fast. Some are even trying to be platforms themselves. They claim to allow the construction of decentralized apps. However, when you think a little harder about these things, none of it makes sense. None of the shitcoins show any proof of actual decentralization. Some events in bitcoin's history couldn't have happened if bitcoin hadn't been sufficiently decentralized. The denial of the *SegWit2x* hard fork in 2017 is a clear example of this. Every "inventor" of a "blockchain" after bitcoin must have been aware of bitcoin. Therefore, insider information was always available to all shitcoin creators. Shitcoins are pre-mined and controlled by small, centralized groups of people. None of them can guarantee a fixed supply issuance schedule like bitcoin can. They are all a bigger fool's game, and they contribute nothing to the betterment of mankind. Bitcoin, on the other hand, definitely does. Bitcoin is deflationary in the long run. Deflation is always advertised as a bad thing by those who run the money printers. This is the greatest lie ever told. In truth, a deflationary monetary base layer is the only thing that can save humanity from itself. By giving people an incentive to save rather than spend, we stop the vicious cycle of consumerism. It ends the "fairytales of perpetual growth" that certain teenage climate activists like to talk about every now and then.

The other shitcoin subcategory is Kleptocurrency. We all use Kleptocurrencies, or fiat money, the more common term for these scams. No issuer of money has ever been able to resist the temptation of enriching himself via excess printing. Inflation cannot happen without an increase in the money supply. If money couldn't be created out of thin air and handed out as loans, inflation wouldn't exist. Gold remained a first layer type of money for over 5000 years because of its natural properties. Gold is scarce and uncommon in nature. It is also relatively easy to verify the authenticity of gold. Biting on the coin was one way of confirming it was made of the real deal. As mentioned in the prelude to this book, something happened when banking was introduced to the world. When banking was first invented, the bankers soon realized something. That they could hand out more receipts for gold than they actually held in their vaults. The probability of every customer withdrawing all their gold at once was very low. This is how the first monetary bill came to be. It enriched the banker at the expense of everyone else. The name of this practice is "fractional reserve banking," and it's still in use today. In fact, it is much worse nowadays.

Since 1971 the world's current reserve currency, the US dollar, has not been redeemable for gold at all. Instead, we're supposed to accept its value by decree. On a website called *WTF Happened in 1971*,[1] numerous graphs and diagrams depict the devastating effects this has had on the US economy since then. Central institutions create all fiat currencies. They contrived a mechanism for funneling wealth from the masses and into the hands of the elite. It is this machine that bitcoin provides a way out of. If you don't find the idea of being a cog in someone else's machine very attractive, you now have a way out. Big governments in cahoots with big corporations rule the world. And they grow more powerful every second because they have access to the most destructive weapon ever invented. A weapon of mass destruction far more dangerous than the atomic bomb. The money printer.

Around 90 percent of all bitcoins that will ever exist are already mined. And everyone knows bitcoin's issuance schedule. So let's call bitcoin deflationary for now, for argument's sake. When you think about it, there can only be one deflationary currency. The introduction of a second one would be an act of inflation in itself. Adding new monetary units never adds value, regardless of what you call these new units. Also, it always dilutes the value of the units that already exist. This is true not only for money but for everything.

---

[1] https://wtfhappenedin1971.com/

Economics only applies to scarce goods. Things in abundance are free because their supply greatly exceeds the demand. The air you breathe is an example of such goods.

Understanding this concept is crucial to understanding bitcoin. This is why it's so important to view bitcoin as a discovery rather than an invention. You cannot solve the double-spending problem twice. Solving it again would be double-spending in itself. The discovery made was the discovery of a deflationary base layer of money. THE deflationary base layer. This could only happen once. The circular shape is the best geometric shape for constructing a wheel, and it could only be discovered once. Bitcoin is the best form of money because it solved the double-spending problem and was a one-time discovery.

Deflation is portrayed as a bad thing by Keynesian economists. In Keynesian economic theory, spending is the most critical metric. The leading idea of this economic school claims that spending is a good thing. Every time a dollar bill is being exchanged for something, you add that dollar's value to the entire economy. This is what Keynesians believe. They leave out that you can't create value by printing dollar bills. A dollar bill spent only adds value to the economy if spent on investment. Consumer goods don't add anything to the real economy. They only add to the world's ever-growing garbage piles. Another name for the number of times a dollar gets used per unit of time is "velocity of money." Keynesians view this as the most important metric there is. They're right in the sense that an economy with no monetary velocity at all would stand still and not grow. But there is no evidence that a single global deflationary currency would lead to such a slow down. Deflation is often described as the cause of decreasing monetary velocity in an economy. When everyone is hoarding money, that money isn't put to use. That is the theory.

But bitcoin solves this problem in two ways. In one way now, and another post hyperbitcoinization. The incentive to spend bitcoin now comes from its increased purchasing power. If you've held on to your bitcoins for a mere five years, you've experienced ten thousand percent gains. Few can resist selling off some after a ride like that. Post hyperbitcoinization, monetary velocity seems trickier. Why would anyone sell the best asset to ever exist? The answer is that momentum will come from necessity. Hyperbitcoinization happens when we all demand to get paid in bitcoin. Not when we choose to sell them. When everyone on Earth requires payment in bitcoin, the coins will have to circulate. You will have no choice but to shrink your stack every now and then. Everyone will have to spend at least some to survive.

An obvious tip here is to start demanding to get paid in bitcoin right now. Chances are that the sooner you do so, the more money you'll make. The best time to earn a bitcoin is always yesterday since it was easier then. The next best time is always now. This is a race, and you have a head start already. What are you waiting for? Start working for bitcoin right now! Think about what alternatives you have. More inflation, more debt, more government interference. More prohibitions, more surveillance, more "public" property. More misallocation of resources, more dependency on the state for your survival. In short, more high time preference decisions and more fear. An entity with ultimate power will never give up that power voluntarily. It is naive to think that it will. What team you choose to vote for doesn't matter at all in this regard. You have to reclaim the driver's seat on your own if you truly want it back.

Many movies detail the timeless saga of a person or a small group of people regaining their freedom from a tyrannical government, a lord, a boss, or a dictator. A good flick needs a good villain, and my favorite movies all have charismatic villains in them. Antagonists often drive the motives of all other characters by instilling fear in them. In some films, the antagonist is the main character. In others, the lead character starts out as a protagonist but morphs into the villain during the movie. A well-written villain is a great storytelling tool. In a classic good-versus-evil story, the bad guy's actions motivate the hero to act. This moves the story forward. "The Dark Knight" is an excellent example of such a movie. In a good-guy-turning-evil-type tale, we see the hero change because of incentives. "Scarface" is a perfect example of this type of story structure.

On the whole, a compelling villain is often what separates a mediocre movie from a good one. But what roles do villains play in real life? We human beings tell ourselves stories. We imagine our lives as ongoing movies or novels. We look upon moving to a new house, getting a new job, or having children as the beginning of a new chapter. We see ourselves as the main character in the movie of our life. We're the protagonist, and we're on a journey. The music we love becomes the soundtrack of the movie. Our friends become sidekicks and comic relief characters. This is an effect that movies and books have on our psyches and the stories we construct. Movies are the way they are because we are the way we are. We tell stories the way we do because of how we experience time. Our lives have a beginning, a middle, and an end. In a way, we are on a "hero's journey," whether we like it or not. We all have a limited amount of time, and we all need to choose one action over another as we go about our daily lives. What our lives often lack, though, is a charismatic villain.

So what do we do to fill this void in times of peace? We're already on top of the food chain. We're already in an environment where we don't have to fight for our own survival very often. So we invent villains. Or have them created for us. Politicians, in particular, love to devise new threats. To make our life stories a little more interesting. We vilify our opponents in sports, religion, and almost every other aspect of life. The media loves this. We have biases in our brains that make us register negative news more than positive ones. Social media platforms amplify people's differences. They let users shield themselves from opinions that don't align with what they believe is true. Every viewpoint not shared by the "other side" becomes "fake news." The world seems markedly more polarized now than it did a decade ago. We all seem to forget that other human beings aren't the enemy. Bad ideas are. We're all humans, and we all act because of our incentives to do so. If a political system is corrupt at its core, people will act in dishonest ways.

Bitcoin doesn't need a central bank antagonist to survive and thrive. No one is forcing anyone to do anything in bitcoin. It's all about cooperation. Defending an opinion is not the same as arguing against its counter-opinion. Showing other people the benefits of a new idea is often more productive than debating its critics. Bitcoiners are not politicians and don't need to be. We don't have to attack our opponents to win. The real antagonist lives within us. Our short-sighted temptations are often a more significant threat to our well-being than people we disagree with. As Franklin D. Roosevelt put it, "There's nothing to fear but fear itself." Keep this in mind at all times, and you'll have a much better shot at getting somewhere in life. Your ego is your own worst enemy. Your own biased view of how things ought to be is the biggest obstacle you'll ever have to overcome. You, and your biases, are the most option-limiting force you'll ever encounter in life.

As mentioned earlier, the digital realm is nothing but ones and zeroes at its core. Everything digital is binary information. Everything on a computer is a string of ones and zeroes. This makes it very easy for computers to replicate all information. As a matter of fact, a computer cannot send data without copying it first. When thinking about money on the internet, or digital cash, you soon realize that this poses a problem. A big problem. How can you ensure that your digital money isn't sent twice? This is the double-spending problem. It is the most crucial problem that bitcoin solves. One could even say that bitcoin's fixed supply cap is a side effect of the solution to this problem. Traditional fiat currencies have trusted third parties, ensuring that double-spending doesn't happen. Well, they say they do, but it's a bit more complicated in reality. Banks don't double-spend, but they do inflate the money supply. Fiat currencies are inflationary. This means that they get conjured into existence out of thin air. A very sneaky way of double-spending by diluting the value of the money in your account. But it is double-spending. Don't mistake it for anything else. If prices are going up, your money is being double-spent.

Bitcoin introduced a new way of solving the double-spending problem. Without trust in a single third party. It did this by introducing the Proof-of-Work blockchain. A distributed ledger that contains all bitcoin transactions. Every participant in the network validates what's going on at all times. Bitcoin miners look for new bitcoins and find them in blocks every ten minutes. On average, it takes ten minutes to find a new block, regardless of the total energy expended by miners. The miner that finds the new block gets a reward in the form of a predetermined certain amount of bitcoin in addition to all the transaction fees paid. That's where new bitcoins come from.

But there's more to the double-spending problem than this. What if there's a change to the protocol rules at some point? Can't the rules change so that someone can double-spend or inflate the supply in the future? Bitcoin's protocol rules are extremely tough to change.

Almost every user needs to agree that changing the rules is a good idea for a change to happen. What a bitcoin is gets determined by what program people choose to run on their computers. In late 2017, a specific event proved that the network's users were the ones in charge of it. A proposed upgrade to the protocol called SegWit, which most users wanted, was on the table.

SegWit is short for Segregated Witness. Most bitcoin companies also wanted the upgrade. But only if the amount of data each block could contain was increased to two megabytes instead of one. These companies banded together in New York and decided they wanted both upgrades. First Segregated Witness via a backward-compatible soft fork. Then a doubling of the block size via a non-backward compatible hard fork. Hard forks can implement any change to a protocol but force the network to split. Soft forks are more limited, but they keep the network together and do not force users to run the new code. Segregated Witness, which the users wanted, was implemented shortly after the meeting in New York. But the hard fork never happened because the users refused it. This revealed that the big companies weren't in charge of bitcoin. The users were. A block size increase would have been detrimental to the network. It would have increased the total size of the blockchain, making it more costly for the average Joe to run a full node.

Moreover, it would have set a precedent for increasing it again in the future. It would have made bitcoin centralized. In other words, bitcoin would not have been a solution to the double-spending problem. A centralized digital currency is no better than a central bank-issued one. This event is now remembered as a pivotal point in bitcoin's history. To many bitcoiners, yours truly included, the turn of events in 2017 was critical. It proved that bitcoin worked since it couldn't be hijacked by even the most powerful cartel.

The double-spending problem is more complex than it seems. A blockchain solves some technical aspects, but there's more to the double-spending problem than that. The problem isn't solved if the blockchain's rules can be easily changed. An argument can be made that bitcoin doesn't solve it either since no one knows what will happen in the future. But bitcoin has proven robust enough to counter all attacks against it for more than twelve years. And it has been attacked a lot, from all sorts of imaginative vectors, technical and social. Bitcoin persists because of its uncompromising users. You know, the toxic bitcoin maximalists. They are its immune system. In bitcoin, every user knows about the 21 million coin supply cap and how integral it is to the functionality of the network. A sufficient number of node owners know about the protocol's other ironclad foundations. They ensure that it won't ever "upgrade" into something disastrous.

Yet, an economic aspect of the problem is often overlooked. Money is, by definition, the most saleable good in society. The thing that is easiest to sell for other things. Bitcoin is the only type of money with a guaranteed fixed supply cap. If we don't want our coins to be double-spent, we shouldn't use any other kind of money. Doing so is double-spending, in a way. This might seem far-fetched, but hear me out. Now that we have bitcoin, we have a type of money with a fixed supply. Whenever we choose to use something other than bitcoin as money, we're not helping each other. Whatever we used that money for, we're not letting its value funnel into the total value of bitcoin. When we choose to accept other things as payment, we're not helping Bitcoin reach its full potential. Everything, divided by 21 million.

Every trade that does not involve bitcoin or barter enables double-spending. It happens via inflation in one way or another. Some invisible third party is leeching value off the money you use. In this sense, inflation is double-spending. Every time the money supply increases, the issuer double-spends a part of your wealth. This dilution of the value of your money is a type of double-spending. Someone who isn't you is enjoying the fruits of your labor. An infinite amount of inflationary currencies can exist at the same time. But there can only be one deflationary currency. An additional one would defeat its own purpose. Absolute scarcity in a digital asset is resistance to replicability. A successful copy of bitcoin would dilute bitcoin's value. This is why they all fail sooner or later. You can only solve the double-spending problem once. Solving it again would be double-spending. Bitcoin is the chance we've got. There won't be a second chance. Whenever you use it, you help a nonviolent world become a reality.

Living with a deflationary world reserve currency will be weirder than we can envision. Imagine the world post hyperbitcoinization and after the last bitcoin has been mined. No one on Earth accepts anything other than bitcoin as payment for all goods and services. The total amount of bitcoins in circulation can only go down at this point. This means that most people's stacks necessarily have to decrease in size over time. There's a catch, though. The purchasing power of each bitcoin will still be going up. This means that even though people's stacks might be diminishing, their purchasing power can increase. A good business is a business that profits in real purchasing power terms over time. This means that companies can hold diminishing bitcoin stacks and still be profitable.

What will matter is the rate of loss in bitcoin terms. It is difficult to imagine what living in such a world will be like. Another Unit of Account than bitcoin will probably have to exist at this point. Measuring prices in bitcoin will be too different from what we're used to.

Kilowatt-hours might be it. Electrical energy is directly connected to bitcoin but could match other prices better. Kilowatt-hour prices could help us wrap our heads around the ever-decreasing costs of the new world economy. They could provide us with some price stability, the oh, so sought-after property of money in the fiat world we live in today. Kilowatt-hours could allow us to keep the cake and eat it too. Price stability in a world where the monetary base layer is deflationary.

10

ADOPTION

I N many computer games, the character you play has two primary resources to spend, health and mana. Your mana is the resource you spend when casting spells or using abilities. When your mana is depleted, your ability to interact with the world around you becomes limited. You usually have to rest or consume some form of mana replenishing potion when this happens. Your health points serve a more obvious purpose as you usually die and respawn at some inn or resurrection location when you run out of health. Now, why health and mana? Probably because they align very well with the resources you have at hand in your real life. Your health points are akin to the time you have left on this Earth, and your mana is akin to your energy. Money is supposed to be a mana replenishing potion, and the only type of money that fulfills this function is bitcoin. All the other mana potion flasks and bottles are leaking. Like in a computer game, players will eventually figure out which potion works better for them. Players who figure this out more quickly will be rewarded accordingly. The same is true for bitcoin. Life is like a computer game, and those who figure out which of the game's items best serves them will progress faster. The sooner you adopt bitcoin, the more you stand to gain. Most people think that this effect will end at some point, but they're missing the point. Bitcoin's purchasing power is designed to go up forever.

When a new technology disrupts an old one, adoption usually happens in an S-shaped fashion. Especially when it comes to networked technologies. This is because of a phenomenon called *Metcalfe's Law*. The number of connections increases in proportion to the square of the number of users. Thus, universal adoption of a new network technology starts slow and expands fast. In other words, the adoption rate is exponential. Exponentiality is hard for the human mind to comprehend.

Furthermore, the value of the network derives from the number of connections. Not the number of users. As the network approaches its user limit, its adoption curve smoothes out again. Imagine a graph with the number of users on its Y-axis and time on its X-axis. Network adoption usually looks like an "S" on such a graph. The radio, the telephone, the TV, the PC, the internet, Google, and Facebook all had S-shaped adoption curves. Also, the process was more rapid for each subsequent communication network. The more connected we are, the faster new communications networks can propagate.

Because of this, the dominant theory about bitcoin's adoption is that the price of bitcoin will "stabilize" at some point. But it might not be correct. The thesis might be wrong due to our innate inability to understand exponentials. "The greatest shortcoming of the human race is our inability to understand the exponential function," as Professor Albert Allen Bartlett once so eloquently put it. There's a high probability that bitcoin's future price development will prove Professor Bartlett right. Bitcoin's user base may have an S-shaped adoption, sure. But its value, that's another story. Bitcoin's valuation curve could have the shape of a "J" rather than an "S" for a very long time. The fundamental reason is that you always have to measure value relative to something else. This is especially true for money. Money is the most universal good in society. This means that we can only estimate the value of other things relative to the value of money. By definition, the most universal trading good in a society becomes its money. Bitcoin, the technology, may have an S-shaped adoption. But bitcoin, the asset, will experience a very different journey. If you're a hodler, you'll share a very similar journey. A trip that might require a seatbelt.

Hyperbitcoinization is the theoretical event in which bitcoin replaces all other money. When everyone stops using their local currency and starts using bitcoin instead. After this point, people will no longer measure bitcoin in dollars but dollars in bitcoin. The thought is hard to wrap your head around as it is. But in reality, the event is even weirder than you can imagine. First of all, there's no endpoint to hyperbitcoinization. It's a continuous process. It begins when people start demanding to get paid in bitcoin for their goods and services. After that, all the money in the world gets absorbed by the bitcoin economy.

With this, the value of everything else will be absorbed by bitcoin too. The world is worth everything that money can buy twice. The money itself is worth just as much. Once the world is on a sound money standard, the world economy will look astonishingly different. What we're living in now has very little in common with what a completely free global market will be like. Right now, money is credit, so there's way more debt than assets around. A hyperbitcoinized world will be a different beast altogether. A world in which almost every human interaction is entirely voluntary. To say that it might be more productive than what we live in now would be the understatement of the century. We all win when we remove violence from the equation and incentivize everyone to think long-term. Such a society will be a lot more efficient and less wasteful at an ever-increasing rate. Imagine all the value derived from this increased efficiency represented by bitcoin. At the same time, bitcoin's supply rate will continue to halve every four years. Nothing can stop this. All the money in the world. An ever more efficient market. A capped supply of bitcoins. Everyone focused on capital accumulation instead of mindless consumption. In other words, infinite progress.

Add to this the exponential developments in robotics and artificial intelligence. In theory, the purchasing power of bitcoin can only go up. Forever. It is beyond mind-blowing. As mentioned earlier, our inability to understand exponentials is our most significant flaw. Bitcoin will prove this. It will sound impossible until it happens. It is already weird, but we haven't seen anything compared to what's about to happen. The old institutions will be obsoleted by the new paradigm. One by one, they will crumble as their "services" will no longer be needed. Empires will fall. The dollar will fall. The earlier you become a sovereign individual, the more you'll enjoy the ride.

Think of hyperbitcoinization in stages. The first stage is personal. You discover bitcoin, become interested, start learning, and so on. Before long, you've opted out of your old life and begun living and breathing bitcoin. The real turning point is when you start accepting nothing but bitcoin as payment. For everything you do. Nothing but bitcoin for all your goods and services. The second stage begins when everyone on Earth goes through the same process. First, everyone acquires some bitcoin. Then, all the money starts flowing into bitcoin. Everyone will realize that the old monetary paradigm is pointless at some point. This is the true beginning of an S-shaped adoption, and we're still far, far away from that here in 2022. But hyperbitcoinization doesn't end there either. After all the fiat currencies are gone, the value of the other assets will start flowing into bitcoin. The value of all the gold, silver, and other precious metals will soon follow. Plus, the value of all the real estate and all the bonds. Everything there is, and everything there ever will be, divided by 21 million.

Tools used to be material things. But most tools today have moved into the informational realm. When they do, their production costs vanish. Think about the apps on your phone. Think about all the things they replace. Watches, calculators, phone catalogs, physical maps, and compasses. Flashlights, GPSs, record players, video cassettes, the weatherman, and all the newspapers. They're all apps on your phone now. This means that their production costs are trending towards zero. Information trends towards its marginal cost of production, zero. Moore's Law is still in play. Moore's Law observes that the number of transistors in dense integrated circuits doubles every two years. In other words, the cost of information halves every two years. Most people have heard of this but have not yet understood its implications. As mentioned in earlier chapters, the primary purpose of all tools and technologies is to save time. Every company on Earth uses technology to deliver better goods to their clients. If they didn't, they would run out of business. Every entrepreneur tries to make life easier for their customers. In other words, they're trying to save people time. And they succeed at an exponential rate. Things are moving so fast that the human mind can't understand what's happening. Two years from now, the production cost of everything will be half of what it is now. Four years from now, a fourth. Six years from now, an eighth. But there is a force pulling in the opposite direction. Inflation. Inflation is preventing this from happening.

The fiat system does not allow for it. Technology and central banking are polar opposites. One is working towards freeing up our time. The other is stealing it. Inflation has to adapt to keep up with the exponentiality of technological progress. It has to get worse in an exponential manner. To achieve "price stability," it will have to cut your purchasing power in half every two years. Monetary inflation is wage deflation. Your salary will buy you fewer goods and fewer services every year unless it doubles every two years. You know this, but your brain cannot realize its true extent. Exponentials aren't intuitive to us. We're simply not wired for them. The saddest part about this is that people will vote for more of what is causing the damage in the first place. The people who suffer the most from all this will vote for more government control. History tells us the same sad story everywhere. Higher salary thresholds, more social security, public healthcare, UBI. Without inflation, governments couldn't afford any of it. To keep the facade up, they need to continue to inflate their national currencies exponentially. Hyperinflation is not just a risk. It is inevitable.

Now there is an upside to all this bad news. As the world enters a more clownish era, the old institutions begin to reveal their true selves. Governments keep imposing more and more severe measures that limit your freedoms depending on how obedient you've been. In doing this, they expose their true nature. They're not here to help and protect you. Their true intention is to control. They want you to be afraid because you will do what you're told when you are. The more time passes, the easier it will become to separate signal from noise, though. As it does, more and more people will realize what's going on. How fooled they've been.

When people do, they discover bitcoin. Bitcoin is an unmistakable lighthouse beacon in an ocean of misinformation. The only way to find a safe shore is by following bitcoin, the beacon. Once you see it, its light will illuminate everything. A credit-based monetary system cannot allow for an accelerating technological deflation. To keep up with that, you must separate your money from the hands of the state. YOU need to, not "we need to." The most dangerous word in the world is "we." The notion of "we need to" got us into this mess in the first place. It is the idea of "we" that funnels wealth from the common man and into the pockets of the elite. A sinister minority is using the gullibility of the ignorant majority to enrich themselves at everyone's expense. To break out of the system, you need to take matters into your own hands.

The beauty of bitcoin is that it's an idea that is powerful enough to make the transition inevitable. The system can't fix the system from within the system. But people will opt out if they can. The lower the cost of producing new money, the higher the prices of everything else. The higher the cost of printing new money, the lower the prices of everything else. Bitcoins are approaching a point of infinite production costs. We bitcoiners have an abundant material future to look forward to. But we won't even crave material things. We will reclaim the ownership of our limited time on this Earth. A far better goal to strive for. Both for the individual and for the planet. The signal becomes more evident every year. Bitcoin can and will increase its purchasing power every year, forever.

Digital payments within the banking system are a surveillance system in disguise. Your spending habits are recorded every time you use your credit- or debit card. KYC and AML laws are making this worse. The old system will lead to a very dystopian future. If we want a hint at what it might look like, we should study what's going on in China. If you jaywalk in some parts of China, you get a fine that your phone pays without your consent. It pays for it twice, in fact. First, you pay the penalty with actual money. Then, you pay it again with a reduction of your social credit score. The social credit score system in China is an example of how dystopic the future can become. It is a way to control the population by rewarding obedience. And punishing disobedience. Hitler and Stalin would have loved it. Total control. Social engineering at its best. The levers in their super villain's lair would control each individual at all times. They wouldn't even need guns!

A system based on theft in the base layer of money must, as a byproduct, drive to increasing control and removal of your personal rights and freedoms. It must do this to protect its thieving rights in the first place. Long-term, you cannot have individual rights in a dishonest, inflationary system. Can democracy survive in a dishonest system? If democracy is based on people's right to choose, but that right to choose is predicated on theft in the base layer of money that must expand exponentially to sustain itself, do the people really have a choice at all? No one votes for having the value of their cash diluted. No one votes for bail-outs. Ask yourself if what you're living is an actual democracy at all. Is democracy even possible in an inflationary system?

The parallel reality that bitcoin creates is happening right now. Today, both McDonald's and Starbucks are forced to accept Lightning payments in El Salvador. These giant global corporations are currently experiencing all the advantages of Bitcoin and the Lightning Network. As they do, they will start advocating for bitcoin everywhere and become a lobbying force to be reckoned with everywhere. And they are just one example. As science fiction writer William Gibson said, "The future is already here — it's just not very evenly distributed." It will be, though, since this is happening everywhere at once in every level of society. The company boards of McDonalds and Starbucks are experiencing it, and so is Joe, the Canadian truck driver. This is happening right now. Look around you. The price of bitcoin has gone up on average by 200% annually since its inception. And it shows no signs of slowing down. Mainstream adoption will happen faster than you think and sooner than you think. It will be weirder than you think, but the transition will probably be smoother because this technology is more powerful than anyone realizes. We are not wired to understand it. The success of Google, Facebook, Apple, and Amazon were events never before seen in human history. But bitcoin is not a company. It has more than one use case. In fact, it has EVERY use case. Money can be exchanged for absolutely everything. Neither you nor anyone else is prepared for what's coming. Get off zero. Make your friends and family get off zero. You won't regret it.

One obvious use case for bitcoin is cross-border payments. Currency conversion and settlement can be done instantly using the Lightning Network. Any sum of money can now be sent between jurisdictions, without any rent-seeking middlemen, instantly and without cost. This effectively means that remittances are now free, regardless of what anyone in the world thinks of that fact. Money is now a language in every sense of the word. Sending money and sending a text message is now the same thing. A mere twenty years ago, sending a text message or making a call to another continent was extremely expensive. The price per megabyte was enormous. Today, we can communicate via video link with people on the other side of the globe, instantly and without cost. To try to charge people for text communication alone in 2022 seems preposterous. Now imagine streaming money. This is an actual upgrade to the internet. A massive upgrade, and it's already here. Logic gates and circuits made electronics and hence computers possible. Who knows what value gates and circuits will lead to? The possibilities are endless.

You use the internet whenever you pay for anything with a credit- or debit card. These networks are built on internet protocols. Bitcoin is, among many other things, an internet protocol. Like TCP/IP became the dominant protocol for transferring data, "HFSP/BTC,"[1] or whatever we may call it in the future, will be the dominant protocol for value transfer. Everything can be built on top of this base layer. Even applications for traditional fiat currencies. Telecommunications companies tried to fight innovation for a while, but nowadays, all telephone calls are made over the internet.

The same will happen to the remittance market. It is a trivial expense to send a sum of bitcoin to any other country in the world over the Lightning Network. As long as the bitcoins can be converted into fiat instantly in both countries (which they can), there's no reason for any remittance service to use any other protocol. The Lightning Network is instant, global, and almost free. Its fees for sending and receiving bitcoin are so low that they're negligible, especially compared to legacy services. And all the infrastructure needed is already in place. It is only a matter of time before all the world's monetary transactions run on the Lightning Network. Google, Facebook, and Amazon all run on Linux servers. This tells the layman that those who know what they're doing prefer open-source software. There's no reason to think that people won't use the perfect protocol for value transfer now that it's here. The Lightning Network is still the world's most underrated invention. Like Bonnie Tyler once put it: "We're living in a powder keg and giving off sparks." Bitcoin is the keg, and the Lightning Network is the spark generator. Bitcoin is about to blow up. Prepare accordingly.

---

[1] HFSP stands for "Hashed Final Settlement Protocol."

11

TRANSITION

W E live in a world where technology drives down the costs of everything at a jaw-dropping rate every day. We also live in a world where the current monetary paradigm cannot allow deflation. This cannot be stressed enough. Deflation which in itself, is a natural phenomenon. Inflation is not. Prices ought to go down because we get better at doing stuff all the time. As discussed earlier, that's what technology is. Technology saves us time. It is deflationary in its nature. Prices ought to reflect this, but they don't. In other words, we aren't saving time. This is because the money in your bank is not money. It is credit. Every unit of fiat currency is a credit owed by someone to someone. The entire system runs on credit, not capital. It has to inflate. There is never enough money in the system, and there never will be. This means that the system has to create more and more credit every year. To sustain itself, it funnels more and more wealth away from you and into the hands of your overlords. It could not function if it didn't. As the system becomes more fragile over time, world leaders have to impose more and more control over their populations. To make us obey, they have to make us fear something. "The urge to save humanity is almost always a false front for the urge to rule," as H.L.

Mencken put it back in his day. Fear keeps populations in check. But not forever. Inflationary systems are not stable. They have to collapse sooner or later.

Money should be a representation of human time. Tools and technologies' primary purpose is to save us time. This should result in the ever dropping prices of all goods and services. But the prices go up instead. The only reason they do is that the system itself is stealing your time. I cannot stress this enough. You are being robbed all the time. What's even worse is that you did this to yourself. You've been using pieces of paper and numbers on a screen all your life, thinking it was money. It never was. It was credit all along, designed to steal your time. You got punked by your banker. In a very embarrassing way. If you've managed to get your hands on a couple of tangible assets, good for you. They're the only things that can provide you with an airbag when the crash comes. Those who don't own any assets are paying for the whole charade. Being poor is very expensive.

Think of it this way — what would the world look like if someone could corrupt time itself? In doing this, you soon realize that this is the world you live in today. Every hamster has to spend more and more hours per day on the wheel. At the same time, it is becoming impossible for that same hamster to ever afford his own home. Politicians gain more power while focusing on more arbitrary issues all the time. The virus. The climate. Immigration. Gender inequality. Terrorism. The wage gap. If the underlying problem isn't addressed first, these issues are pointless to discuss. The only real problem is dishonest money.

Few people realize how true this is. You can't cure cancer with a band-aid. There's no getting around this. Inflation is theft. Even if you believe in democracy, you still didn't vote for inflation, nor did anyone else. And inflation must exist in a credit-based monetary system. Credit-based financial systems must grow forever by design and are thus inherently unsustainable. Most people don't even question the legitimacy of inflation but think it's a necessity. We're led to believe that it's a necessary part of a functioning economy. A crucial element, even. This is the biggest lie ever told. Think about it. How could mass theft benefit an economy? How can you create more value by printing more pieces of paper? By increasing a number on a screen?

The answer is simple — You can't. Theft doesn't benefit anyone. Not even the thief, given a long enough time frame. Keeping an angry mob equipped with torches and pitchforks at bay can be a very costly thing. So why aren't more people upset about inflation? Why can't they realize what's going on? Those who don't own assets are paying for the whole charade, but very few seem to understand what's going on. The answer lies within the problem itself. Most people don't have the time to think about these things because they live in constant fear. Fear of losing their jobs, fear of not making ends meet, fear of tomorrow. Remember, fear and high-time preference are on the same side of the behavioral spectrum.

This is the true tragedy of the commons. People are bereft of the time they need to realize that a robbery has occurred. We know what this leads to. We know where it ends. History has shown us that several times. It ends in wars and revolutions. Unfortunately, the system itself is never put into question. Humans make the same mistake over and over. Hard men create good times, good times create weak men, weak men create bad times, and bad times create hard men. Unfortunately, this cycle perpetuates itself through inflation. People living in fear are easy to manipulate. Fear is a convenient weapon and tool for the ruling class. They can channel our fear and aim it at a particular part of the population. Every group gets blamed by the other group. The immigrants, the racists, the polluters, the environmentalists. The vaxxers, the anti-vaxxers, the left, the right, the capitalists, the socialists. All these groups are villainized routinely by their opponents. "They" always get the blame. You very seldom hear a politician say, "It's our fault." Politicians who do, don't win elections. Politicians who say, "It's not your fault. It's those people's fault," win. Whoever gets elected will use the same rhetoric to do the same thing repeatedly. They'll print more money to steal your time at an ever-increasing rate. As long as this goes on, politicians won't solve anything. They can't. Those who would be able to will not get elected. They can't.

In his essay "The Basic Laws of Human Stupidity" from 1976, Italian economist Carlo Cibolla explores an unflattering facet of human behavior. These are Cipolla's five fundamental laws of stupidity:

- Always and inevitably, everyone underestimates the number of stupid individuals in circulation.

- The probability that a particular person will be stupid is independent of any other of that person's characteristics.

- A stupid person is a person who causes losses to another person or to a group of persons while deriving no gain and even possibly incurring losses to himself.

- Non-stupid people always underestimate the damaging power of stupid individuals. In particular, non-stupid people constantly forget that at all times and places, and under any circumstances, to deal and/or associate with stupid people always becomes a costly mistake.

- A stupid person is the most dangerous type of person.

He also defines four main categories of people. Stupid people are those whose efforts are counterproductive to their own and others' interests. The opposite of stupidity is intelligence. Cibolla defines the intelligent as "those who contribute to society and leverage their contributions into reciprocal benefits." Then there's the group that contributes to society but gets taken advantage of by that society. Cibola calls this group "the helpless." Boxer, the horse in Orwell's "Animal Farm," is a perfect example of a helpless person. The last group consists of the bandits. These people pursue their own self-interest. Even while doing so poses a net detriment to societal welfare. Cibola argues that bandits are less dangerous than stupid people. We can learn how to tackle bandits since their actions are at the very least predictable. Stupid people's actions are irrational. Bandits follow incentives. Now think about every person you've ever known.

Which category do they fall under and why? By the way, these groupings aren't absolute. For instance, a bandit may enrich himself more or less and harm society to a smaller or a more considerable extent. Also, a naïve person may improve his community more or less than he hurts himself. Some people believe that Cibolla wrote the article as a semi-joke. But approach it from a different angle, and it can explain a lot about the current state of the world. The bandits try to fool other people all the time. But they couldn't do it if there weren't fools around, to begin with. Stupid people not only fall for the trickery of the bandits, but they fool themselves too. And they're everywhere.

Stupidity and bandit-ism have a solid connection to time preference. When you have a high time-preference mindset, you're more likely to make stupid or selfish choices. A bitcoin denominated world won't make people less stupid to some fantastical degree, but it will make silly decisions more costly and intelligent ones more rewarding.

Democratic systems built on top of unsound monetary policies provide the bandits with the means they need to reach their selfish ends. Mass-theft justified by the votes of throngs of stupid people who fail to see their elected leaders for what they are. Incompetence is the real trickle-down economy. If bandits can put a moron in charge of an institution and avoid scrutiny by doing so, they will. As long as they get the votes, they care about little else. Politicians who prioritize things other than votes don't end up getting elected. Said moron will then poison the entire functionality of that institution by hiring the wrong people. This is the curse of every "public sector" institution. They grow like cancer since they lack the immune system of the free market. It is not costly for them to fail. In some cases, their budgets increase precisely because they fail to deliver on their promises. Spending someone else's money is much easier than spending your own.

"The Fourth Turning" is a book by William Strauss and Niel Howe from 1997. It describes a recurring generation cycle in human societies. It depicts a four-stage social or mood eras cycle. These are the four stages according to Strauss' and Howe's book:

The High, during which institutions are strong, and individualism is weak. Society is confident about where it wants to go collectively, though those outside the majoritarian center often feel stifled by conformity.

The Awakening, during which institutions are attacked in the name of personal and spiritual autonomy. People suddenly tire of social discipline when society reaches its high tide of public progress. They want to recapture a sense of self-awareness, spirituality, and personal authenticity. Young activists look back at the previous High as an era of cultural and spiritual poverty.

The Unraveling is the opposite of a High: institutions are weak and distrusted, while individualism is strong and flourishing. Highs come after Crises when society wants to coalesce and build and avoid the death and destruction of the previous Crisis. Unravelings come after Awakenings when people wish to atomize and enjoy.

The Crisis is an era of destruction, often involving war or revolution, in which institutional life is destroyed and rebuilt in response to a perceived threat to the nation's survival. After the Crisis, civic authority revives, cultural expression redirects towards community purpose, and people locate themselves as members of a larger group.

Post-apocalyptic author G. Michael Hopf once described the same phenomenon in one sentence. "Hard times create strong men, strong men create good times, good times create weak men, and weak men create hard times."

Paired with Cibolla's theory of stupidity, we notice a fascinating pattern. Which of Cibolla's four stupidity quadrants is dominant during which era? The first era, or The High, is an age of relative peace and prosperity. But it's also an era when "those outside the majoritarian center often feel stifled by the conformity." In other words, an era in which those in power frown upon creativity. A time when the intelligent rule alongside the bandits and the helpless do what they're told. The bandits and the wise keep the stupid in check to a large extent. This is the era in which strong men try to create good times. But it might not be the best time for entrepreneurs. Institutions grow more prominent during this time and often stifle innovation in the process. The next phase is The Awakening. Here, both the intelligent and the stupid start questioning the status quo. Cracks in the social machinery start to show. The so-called good times create weak men. Individuals without purpose. In this era, the numbers begin to show.

The stupids are revealed to be the largest group in society. Those who don't realize how lucky they are. In relative peace and prosperity, the masses start debating superficial things. They begin questioning the institutions, but for the wrong reasons. Arbitrary issues become important to them. People's preferred pronouns, for instance. This leads to stage three, The Unravelling.

There's a high chance that the era we're currently living in is the tail end of the Unraveling or the beginning stages of Crisis. The fourth turning. Intelligent people are starting to question the old institutions. The internet provides us with new ways of organizing ourselves. Wise people find clever new ways to interact with one another. At the same time, conspiracy theories flourish, and arbitrary issues upset people everywhere. Both Q-anon on the right and Black Lives Matter on the left in America are perfect examples of this. Angry mobs on each side of the political aisle whose primary goal is to create more chaos. Disrupting the established order for whatever reason they see fit. Looting and pillaging in the name of some misguided cause. Those upset about immigrants or pronouns start to form militias. A mass flight of intelligence ensues. Today, bitcoiners are fleeing the EU and the US for more freedom-oriented places. They do so because they see what's coming. The Fourth Turning. The Crisis.

Could we avoid outright war during the Crisis this time around? Bitcoin might be the tool we need to break the vicious cycle of the four turnings. A tool for empowering the intelligent and disempowering the bandits while at the same time providing a much more stable environment for the helpless. The stupids are hard to help. But society ought to function in a way that prevents them from getting into positions of power. You can't stop a stupid person from doing stupid things, but you can lessen the impact those stupid decisions have on other people. Bitcoin disincentivizes unethical behavior and thereby reduces the number of bandits in society. Most bandits aren't bandits because of free will. The underlying incentive structure in society turns them into bandits over time. Even outright sociopaths would act ethically if moral behavior was in their own best interest. Human society is all about incentives. Every tier of it. Governments bail out banks and pay people not to work through social security. By doing so, they deprive the people on the receiving end of the bail-outs of something fundamental. The ability to learn from their mistakes and become more productive in the future. The market reflects the actual will of the people. Prices tell you whether others think what you're doing is actually worth doing or not. They enable true collaboration. Another thing happens when people and institutions get paid without providing a service sought after by the market. They get an incentive to stay the way they are. If you pay people to be unproductive, more people will be useless. If you bail out banks that waste their clients' money, more banks will waste more money. It is as simple as that. Realizing this is like thinking one move further ahead in a chess game. Despite their simplicity, these insights are pretty uncommon because of the commonality of stupidity.

The fiat monetary system and public education are dumbing us all down. Like the so eloquently illustrated meat grinder in the movie version of Pink Floyd's "The Wall" from 1982, it turns us all into a mash of industrial consumerist voting cattle sludge. Bitcoin, on the other hand, is a refinery. It takes this sludge and separates the more delicate oils from the crude ones by a chemical process. Adding a tiny amount of element zero, the informational element, turns us into individual actors once again. Sovereign beings, capable of taking responsibility for our own actions. No longer lemmings or sheep, but proud lions ready to take on whatever challenges the future may hold. Separated, the division of labor helps us all. Mashed together, there's no human resource allocation mechanism in society. At the very least, it is significantly handicapped.

As contrasted before, man-made robots roam about on Mars, but bandits are still in charge of governing countries. Some doctors can cure cancer, but we still haven't found a way to pay them that doesn't involve theft or coercion. We can video-chat with people on the other side of the globe, but we still have to go into debt to buy the houses our parents built. The only way to change this is by disempowering the existing institutions. A sneaky form of disempowerment. The only way forward is to plant a seed of honesty in the corrupt soil of government interventionism. If you remove the incentive for violence, people will be less violent. If you remove the incentive to steal, you remove theft. Bitcoin gives everyone an incentive to plan ahead for the future. An incentive to cooperate with fellow human beings. An incentive to accumulate capital and make use of it. To build. To thrive. To flourish.

The global debt bubble will soon collapse. We can't know if we have years, months, or weeks left, but we know that it will collapse at some point. It cannot be sustained since the only thing that can keep a fiat economy going is to print more money each year that passes. When the markets collectively realize what's going on, there will be no way of stopping the crash. In early February of 2008, just before the Lehman Brothers collapse and the following global financial crises, the M2 money supply of the US was about 7.5 trillion dollars. Today, 14 years later, it's three times that. In other words, the Fed and their associates have stolen or will steal at least two-thirds of every American's money since the last global recession. Governments all over the globe are doing what they can to cover up what's actually going on behind the curtains, but sooner or later, the house of cards they've created will have to collapse. Luckily, we know how to survive the fall of all empires. We not only have bitcoin. We are bitcoin.

It is important to remember that most people do not know what you know during the transition. Most people haven't read this book, nor any other bitcoin book for that matter. Many people haven't read a single book in their entire lives. We can't expect everyone to grasp all the implications of what's coming. We have to remember to treat other people kindly, with respect. Most people just want to live their lives, go to their day jobs, and mind their own business. They won't be prepared for riots and civil unrest, and they definitely won't be ready for hyperbitcoinization. Be kind to them, try to educate them, and try not to sound arrogant. Arrogance can turn people against you quickly. We're not the first group of people that have lived through a transition like this. Far from it. Many people from the former East block of Europe lived through the fall of the Soviet Union. Most of them found themselves better off on the other side. As will most of us post hyperbitcoinization. But it will require us to be kind and help each other through this. Do what you can for your community and focus on those closest to you. This is the most grassroots revolution ever. It grows from within us. From our souls. Act accordingly.

ABOUT THE AUTHOR

Knut's books are best described as guided meditation that soothe the experienced and tutor the uninitiated in the ways of bitcoin.

Knut used to have a fiat life as a ship captain and now you may choose him as the captain of your bitcoin space ark to navigate the stormy seas of fiat imposition and swells of cognitive dissonance. Grounded in logic and unbound in spirit, Knut offers something for everyone.

We have plenty of pessimism and outright nihilism in the bitcoin scene and Knut, using his quick wit and humor, whips up a fresh gust of positivity and optimism to disperse the clouds of misery, letting the rays of infinite optionality, prosperity and love shine through.

Made in the USA
Las Vegas, NV
27 March 2024

87840202R10089